Tracks and Traces

 Publications Series

General Editor
Paul van der Velde

Publications Officer
Martina van den Haak

Editorial Board
Wim Boot (Leiden University); Jennifer Holdaway (Social Science Research Council); Christopher A. Reed (The Ohio State University); Anand A. Yang (Director of the Henry M. Jackson School of International Studies and Chair of International Studies at the University of Washington); Guobin Yang (Barnard College, Columbia University).

The *ICAS Publications Series* consists of Monographs and Edited Volumes. The Series takes a multidisciplinary approach to issues of interregional and multilateral importance for Asia in a global context. The Series aims to stimulate dialogue amongst scholars and civil society groups at the local, regional and international levels.

The International Convention of Asia Scholars (ICAS) was founded in 1997. Its main goals are to transcend the boundaries between disciplines, between nations studied, and between the geographic origins of the Asia scholars involved. ICAS has grown into the largest biennial Asia studies event covering all subjects of Asia studies. So far five editions of ICAS have been held respectively in Leiden (1998), Berlin (2001), Singapore (2003), Shanghai (2005), Kuala Lumpur (2007) and Daejeon, South Korea (2009). ICAS 7 will be held in Honolulu from 30 March-3 April 2011.

In 2001 the *ICAS secretariat* was founded which guarantees the continuity of the ICAS process. In 2004 *the ICAS Book Prize* (IBP) was established in order to create by way of a global competition both an international focus for publications on Asia while at the same time increasing their visibility worldwide. Also in 2005 the *ICAS Publications Series* were established.

For more information: www.icassecretariat.org

Tracks and Traces

Thailand and the Work of Andrew Turton

Edited by
Philip Hirsch and **Nicholas Tapp**

AMSTERDAM UNIVERSITY PRESS

 Publications Series

Edited Volumes 13

Cover design: JB&A raster grafisch ontwerp, Westland
Layout: The DocWorkers, Almere

ISBN   978 90 8964 249 3
e-ISBN   978 90 4851 287 4
NUR   761

© ICAS / Amsterdam University Press, Amsterdam 2010

Table of Contents

List of Tables, Figures, and Photographs

Tables

Figures

Photographs

Acknowledgements

We would first like to acknowledge the kind assistance and collaboration of Craig Reynolds, senior historian of classic and modern Thai studies, who helped to organise the conference panel at which these papers first emerged. While ploughing an independent path, Reynolds' research trajectory has several times intersected with Turton's in a mutually respectful and sympathetic way, and Thai studies has greatly benefited from such accommodations across disciplines and world views.

We should like to thank the Australian National University and the University of Sydney for facilitating our attendance at the conference where the majority of these papers were originally presented. We also pay respects to Thammasat University which, with its well-deserved reputation for liberal views, welcomed this panel together with others dealing with such subjects as the free press and the role of the monarchy in Thailand at a time of considerable political turmoil and unrest.

We should thank all those who participated in this panel and contributed papers later, who despite their very varied academic, political and disciplinary backgrounds, felt able to contribute simultaneously to studies of Andrew Turton's work and studies of Thailand. A debt of gratitude is owed to Professor Paritta Chalermpow Koantakool, Director of the Princess Maha Chakri Sirindhorn Anthropological Centre in Thailand, who acted as moderator for our opening discussions. That willingness to participate is in itself a huge tribute to the importance of Andrew Turton's work on Thailand, and in a sense demonstrates the inextricability of his contributions to the modern development of Thai studies.

Of course our tributes are due above all to Andrew, who without ever wishing to be elevated to some pedagogical position of authority, has nevertheless encouraged and enabled so many Thai and non-Thai students in critically appraising the dynamic nature of Thai society in a global era. In this respect, the editors of this volume owe a career-length vote of thanks to our respected *Achaan*.

Philip Hirsch and Nicholas Tapp

SOAS conference group picture, 1988. *Back two rows:* Andrew Turton, Jonathan Rigg, Shigeharu Tanabe, Chatthip Nartsupha, Ian Brown, Nidhi Aeusriwongse, Philip Stott, Jeremy Kemp, Craig Reynolds, Han ten Brummelhuis, Gawin Chutima, Viggo Brun, Henry Ginsburg, David Smyth. *Front row:* Manas Chitakasem, Ruth McVey, Hong Lysa, Utong Prasasvinitchai, Akira Takahashi.

Introduction

Philip Hirsch and Nicholas Tapp

How are scholars shaped by their times, experiences, political inclinations and other dimensions of the contexts in which they are studying and writing? What are the legacies of influential individual scholars as contexts change but their writings and teachings remain etched on the printed page and in the minds of their students, followers and critics? And what is the continuing or residual relevance of social science scholarship of a generation ago in as rapidly changing a society and academic environment as Thailand?

In this collection, we address these key questions in the field of Thai studies through the wide-ranging, some would even say eclectic, anthropology of one scholar – Andrew Turton. The intent of the volume is not to review, summarise, laud or critique one scholar's work *per se*. Rather, it is to address the question of how ideas produced at a particular time reflect on that time, the differences and continuities between that time and the present, and the potentials of scholars and scholarship of one generation to transcend and adapt into the next.

In the chapters that follow, and through a series of reflections on key themes and key writings of Turton, some prominent scholars of Thailand make a number of links between various aspects of Turton's diverse anthropological writing and current scholarship and politics in Thailand. Despite the recognised influence of different strands of his scholarship, and perhaps because of its diversity and the extent to which it has been a product of its times, Turton's body of scholarship has not been considered as a whole, nor has there been a coherent reflection on how it has worked its way into subsequent scholarship on Thailand. The same could be said of a number of scholars and social scientists whose work informs a similar breadth of scholarship in any one of a number of country contexts, so why Andrew Turton and why Thailand?

Andrew Turton, who retired in 2004 from the School of Oriental and African Studies (SOAS), University of London, has for many years been a leading light and inspiration to younger generations of Thai scholars, activists and others working on Southeast Asian issues. His work has covered diverse fields of anthropological economics and ritual. Issues of power and its representations have been key in this work, relating to matriliny, gender and kinship; political economy – class, state, local, supra-village, political process, violence and illegality; slavery, ethnicity and social identity, minority and state; agrarian socio-economic relations and change; social development, social change and popular participation; ideology, culture, local knowledge; practice and discourse; ethnography of modern diplomatic missions; non-academic anthropology and pre-modern vernacular architecture. In other words, Turton's writings have spanned an exceptional range of themes relevant to late twentieth century Thailand and potentially of continuing relevance.

As an activist scholar, Turton is a more complex product of his times than many less engaged academics. With a biography that spans either side of the turmoil of the 1970s that marked what many see as Thailand's fundamental political schism, and with a written output whose first peak coincided with the events around and subsequent to the military coup of 6 October 1976, Turton as a person and as an author is embroiled in that country's recent political history. In part because it was situated temporally between his earlier establishment role as British Council representative and his later writing on the ethnography of encounters by early diplomatic missions (Turton 1997; 1999; 2001; Grabowsky & Turton 2003; see Grabowsky, this volume), this period of his scholarship has been characterised as his 'red period', with an implication that this was relatively short-lived, although Reynolds in this volume questions the ephemerality of such a rubric. But what is undeniable is that the conflicts and values of the time shaped key aspects of Turton's writing and, by implication, this raises important questions about its continuing relevance and influence a generation on, which we believe this volume addresses.

Turning to the question of why we choose to focus on scholarship on Thailand, this collection situates Turton's work not just within its country context but within that particular scholarly space of area studies known as 'Thai Studies'. Thai Studies has for many years been prominently represented by the triennial International Thai Studies Conference, which began through meetings with South Asian scholars in the early 1980s. The notion of 'Thai Studies' itself has often tended to represent an image of Thailand as a homogeneous society with a unified history and a united population. Over the years it has become more and more apparent how increasingly misleading this image is. Thailand is, of course, a complex society with a number of alternative histories and social tendencies all pulling in often quite contrary directions (cf. Bowie 2000; Thongchai 2000). Turton's work has been fundamental in bringing about an awareness of this shift, and it is therefore quite fitting that we should be able to offer this volume regarding his work and influence out of a panel which was organised by the editors, together with Craig Reynolds, at the 10th International Thai Studies Conference at Thammasat University in January of 2008.

The papers in this book tease out Turton's relevance, influence and links to the work of others – including his contemporaries, students and today's generation of Thai scholars – in some of his key writings. Each paper draws on a single theme or piece of work and considers how the ideas therein have traveled in the changing world of ideas and events. The contributions overall reflect both the strength and diversity of Turton's influence and the de-centredness and lack of harmony of Thai society itself, in a collection of essays that deliberately focuses neither on the entirety of Turton's work nor solely on the nature of Thai society, but rather on aspects of Thai society and culture as understood in the light of some of the works of Turton. For example, an outstanding piece is his paper on the limits of ideological domination in Thai society (Turton 1984), to which many of the contributors refer in tracking some of the contours of the current situation in Thailand.

The extent to which such a collection must be a partly fragmentary and diverse one does no more than reflect the nature of Thai society as some of us have come to understand it in the light of this very wide-reaching work. The topics covered here – slavery, ideology, political leadership, popular participation, agrarian social structure and development, radical analysis, citizenship and social subjectivity, the role of tradition, ritual power, pre-modern cultural encounters and ethnoregionalism – certainly do not exhaust the range of Turton's writings and interests. In particular, his earlier work on matriliny and his essay on the political symbolism of vernacular architecture remain largely unexamined here, although several of the papers do refer to these (Jamaree, for example, on matrilineal descent cults, Tapp on vernacular architecture). The Select Bibliography of Turton's main works which we have appended at the end of this book will give an idea of what has not been adequately covered here.

Nor is this is a collection that would provide an overview of Thai society as a whole, yet any collection that sought do so must now be deeply suspect, for reasons which the articles in this collection may make apparent. Nevertheless, there are many common themes that reflect the changing nature of Thai society as examined through Turton's work, for example the historical continuation of forms of debt bondage examined by Craig Reynolds as well as the continuing debates on the 'self-sufficiency economy' (Jamaree, Rigg) and the 'community culture' school of thought (Keyes, Jamaree). What the papers do together as a whole, therefore, is provide what we find to be a remarkably revealing insight into the way understandings of Thailand have changed over the past several decades and the crucial role many of Turton's work have played in this change.

Returning to the three key questions set out above that inspire this collection, we are making links between past and present scholarship, tracing the threads that tie together an understanding of Thailand as a dynamic and rapidly changing society. The first part of establishing such links is to examine what is specific to the time of writing. But what is specific is not necessarily or only in the nature of the research subject, for example the class characteristics of peasant society. It is also the assumptions and theoretical framings behind the understandings of the subject. Jonathan Rigg comments on the rather homogeneous representation of the peasantry in Turton's 1980s work on participation. Interestingly, this contrasts with the emphasis on class and conflict within rural Thailand that Glassman brings out as a key theme in Turton's (1978a) article in his co-edited collection *Thailand: Roots of Conflict*, and which we find in Anan and Hirsch's discussion of the neo-marxist political economy that shaped earlier framing of agrarian transformations. Jamaree's contribution points to some hesitancy in Turton's earlier work about the capitalist or pre-capitalist nature of the 'dominant class', while Paul Cohen examines Turton's analysis of 'non-state manifestations of local power'. Charles Keyes' paper also looks at these cultural conceptions of power in the historical context of the 'ethnoregionalism' with which Northeastern villagers have critiqued elite conceptions of dominant power. The papers move generally from issues of power and economy considered in the first four towards three papers concerned with ideology, discourse and participation, before concluding with two papers that are unique in bringing out Turton's sometimes neglected historical contributions, on slavery and diplomatic missions respectively.

The second aspect of linkage is to trace influence through individual scholars who have taken ideas forward, directly or through less direct influence in their own work. It is notable that three of the authors in this volume (Jamaree, Hirsch and Tapp) are Andrew Turton's students – one from Thailand and two non-native scholars. Another four (Anan, Cohen, Keyes, Reynolds) are Turton's contemporaries, whose ideas and writing have developed in parallel with, and at least in part influenced by, Turton's work. Jonathan Rigg, who was a student in the Geography Department at SOAS while Turton was teaching in the Department of Anthropology and Sociology there, went on to become a junior colleague of Turton on the staff. One 'outlier' here is Jim Glassman, whose scholarly activism is so clearly inspired by Turton, and whose impassioned essay in this volume so radically asserts relevance of the social critique of the 1970s to an era in which there is a crisis of confidence in class-based analysis, that he is every bit as much a '*luuk-sit*' (student, or disciple) as those with more immediate connections with the scholar at the centre of our discussion. A second 'outlier' would be Volker Grabowsky, who as a younger colleague of Turton has been inspired by his work and through a highly fruitful research collaboration with him.

A final aspect of tracing the legacy of critical scholarship is to examine how it set the intellectual and political agenda for subsequent debates, and to examine its heuristic significance for the present. The discussion in the chapters that follow on participation, on power, ideology and hegemony suggests a persistence and contemporary relevance of Turton's ideas, notwithstanding a continuing awkwardness in the present-day application of intellectual categories and seemingly naive political optimism that marked the earlier era. And yet, with the reference to Thaksin's Thailand in so many of these essays (Keyes, Cohen, Tapp, Glassman, Jamaree), with discussion of power in a country as divided now – albeit along different lines – as it was during the 1970s, and where scholarship and politics continue to shape each other, where historiographies collide and debates over allowable discourse rage as never before, the salience of Andrew Turton's work remains much more than merely apparent.

1 Opening Reflections:
Northeastern Thai Ethnoregionalism Updated

Charles Keyes

Introduction

On 20 August 2007, the electorate in Thailand was asked to vote on whether to adopt a new constitution that had been drafted under a military-led government. Although the referendum passed with 57% of the total vote, the vote also demonstrated the 'limits of ideological domination', with 44% of the total population of the country not going to the polls and, especially, with 62% of the population of northeastern Thailand voting against this military-backed social contract. I see the vote among northeastern Thai (or *Khon Īsān*) as derived from conceptions of power that contrast with those held by members of the urban middle class or the traditional elite.

Northeastern Thailand has long been home to the largest percentage of rural people in the Thai population. Historically, these people were 'peasants' (*chāo nā*) in that their livelihood was based primarily on the cultivation of wet rice. Today, while most living in the region pursue many economic activities other than rice farming, and while a very large number spend extended periods living and working in the industrial and service sectors of urban Thailand, most still identify themselves as 'villagers' (*chāo bān*) because they remained deeply rooted in kin and communal groups associated with their natal villages. Over two-thirds of Northeasterners share common linguistic and cultural practices that link them with the Lao of lowland Laos. For this reason, I will use the term Thai-Lao interchangeably with Khon Isan to refer to these people.

In his essay on the 'Limits of Ideological Domination and the Formation of Social Consciousness', Andrew Turton demonstrated that in Thailand 'ruling power is maintained through a combination of ideological and violently coercive forms of domination, rather than by morally persuasive, hegemonic leadership' (Turton 1984: 19). In this paper I argue that, even nearly three decades after the events that Turton was primarily concerned with, this conclusion remains true for most Thai-Lao. In particular, I will show that the marked dissent from support of the new constitution in northeastern Thailand was not a consequence of vote buying or political arm-twisting by supporters of former Prime

Minister Thaksin Shinawatra. Rather, I maintain that this vote – as well as the large-scale support of Northeasterners for Thaksin's Thai Rak Thai party in the parliamentary elections of the first years of the 21st century – represents the updating of a distinctive ethnoregional critique of an elite-constructed ideology of national integration that I previously identified as having emerged in the middle of the 20th century. Today, however, this critique is more potent because it is embraced not by traditional peasants but by villagers who are deeply involved in the capitalist economy, and by their kinsmen who make up the overwhelming majority of Bangkok's working class.

In his paper Turton also observed that 'even in cultural products clearly inherited from much earlier times we can discern the making of the people's (peasants') own "selective tradition": in religious and magical texts, proverbs and sayings, ... folk opera, ritual practices ..., forms of social relations at village and local levels, etc' (Turton 1984: 65). Those who still live (at least for periods) in northeastern villages and their kinsmen who work in Bangkok and elsewhere still draw on cultural conceptions of power that are rooted in the Thai-Lao traditions of northeastern Thailand. In other words, I maintain, the 'selective tradition' of Thai-Lao people underlies the conceptions of power held by those from Isan.

Roots of a Thai-Lao Culture of Power

A century ago, at the very beginning of the 20th century, thousands of people living in what is today northeastern Thailand joined the first major 'peasant' uprising in modern Thai history.[1] Rural people living throughout the region became followers of men whom they recognised as being *phū mī bun* – literally, 'those having merit'. That is, they were recognised as having exceptional powers that were understood to be the legacy of their positive *kamma*[2] from previous lives.

The charisma of these men (and they were all males) was manifest in their magical rites and, especially as the revolt grew, their apparent ability to ward off the weapons wielded by the security forces sent from Bangkok. Chatthip interpreted these revolts as having their origin 'in the primitive commune' (Chatthip 1984: 127) and as aiming at the establishment of a 'free peasantry' (1984: 128) without a state.

My own interpretation was rather different. I saw the revolt as a response to a 'crisis of power' that came about because of the extension of the authority of a now centralised Thai state in a frontier region into which French colonial authority was also expanding. 'In the context of an acute political crisis, the peasantry of NE Thailand turned to ideas with which they were intimately familiar – i.e., ideas derived primarily from their Buddhist beliefs' (Keyes 1977: 302). The *phū mī bun* sought to demonstrate that they had the Buddhist charisma to be alternatives to the king of Siam. These beliefs were embedded in ritual practices associated with village *wat* (temple monasteries), in folk operas (*môlam mū*) that contained narratives of mythical and legendary kings and other powerful persons, and in folklore.

For the ruling elite in Bangkok, the belief in *phū mī bun* was deemed to be rooted in the 'stupidity', 'savagery' and 'ignorance' of the people of the Northeast. Official documents referred to the leaders of the movement as *phī bun*, an oxymoron since it combined the term for 'spirit' or 'ghost' with *bun*, a word meaning 'merit' or 'positive karma'[3] According to the ideology that informed the political decisions of the court of King Chulalongkorn (1868-1910), only the king of Siam possessed sufficient *bārāmī* – a more sophisticated word for the *bun* that legitimated the exercise of power – to be ruler. Moreover, King Chulalongkorn demonstrated his charisma through effective actions in extending his power throughout his realm. This was especially manifest in the centralisation of authority and establishment of a uniform bureaucratic order following reforms instituted in 1892 (Tej Bunnag 1977).

The *phū mī bun* uprising in northeastern Thailand early in the 20th century entailed a rejection by people in the region both of the claim of superior charisma on the part of the Siamese king and of the new political system that Bangkok sought to impose on the regime. The uprising did not, however, entail – as Chatthip has argued – an attempt 'to establish a society of village "socialism" free from state power' (1984: 111). Rather, villagers in the region shared with the elite in Bangkok the belief that legitimate power could be exercised only by men with Buddhist charisma. They differed radically from the Bangkok perspective in their belief about who possessed such charisma.

The uprising failed in part because the reputed magical powers of the *phū mī bun* were no match for the Gatling guns – the equivalent of more modern assault rifles – and disciplined military forces that Bangkok deployed to suppress the insurgents. The ultimate failure, however, came about because many of the most revered senior monks in northeastern Thailand eventually convinced their followers that the Siamese monarch did have superior *bārāmī*. This they did because many of them were members of the *Thammayut-nikāi*, the reformed monastic order that had been founded by King Mongkut, King Chulalongkorn's brother, and was headed by Prince Wachiriyan (Vajirañāṇa-varorasa), a monk who was also the brother of King Chulalongkorn.

Although occasional claimants to being *phū mī bun* would arise from time to time in later years, none ever again succeeded in persuading any significant number of people that they were more charismatic than the King of Siam. Ironically, as non-royal members of the military and civilian elite in Bangkok began to become disaffected with absolute monarchism, the people of northeastern Thailand were beginning to view the Thai monarchy as the ultimate source of legitimate power in their world.

Northeasterners embrace parliamentary democracy

In June 1932 some of the disaffected elite succeeded in staging a coup and compelling King Prajadhipok (r. 1924-1935) to accept a constitution (*ratchathammanūn*) which vested ultimate authority of the state in the 'people' (*rātsadôn* or *prachāchon*) who would express their will through 'democratically' (*prachāthipatai*) elected representatives. The 'Promoters' of the 1932 coup did not, however, eliminate the monarchy. By retaining the monarchy, the 'Promoters' created a crisis of power because those who exercise power (*amnāt*) through having been authorised by an elected parliament are not the same as a king who continues to be re-cognised as having charismatic authority.

Following the coup, Prince Bovaradej, who commanded troops based at Khorat in the Northeast, led his troops to challenge the coup makers and to restore the monarchy as the sole source of authority. Although the rebellion was mainly backed by elite royalists, 'it was generally re-cognised ... that the aims of Bovaradej were shared by the more conservative elements throughout the country, and many provincial officials and officers had openly sympathised with the rebels' (Thompson 1941: 81). New research is needed to be able to determine how much support for the rebellion came from the peasantry in northeastern Thailand. There is evidence, nonetheless, that the government made up of the 'Promoters' was concerned about the 'rebelliousness' of the people of the region. In 1934 the government erected the first monument in the post-1932 period to the memory of a woman from Khorat who in the early 19th century demonstrated her support for Bangkok by leading a resistance to forces sent by the Lao king, Cao Anu. Although prior to (and after) 1934, Thāo Suranārī (Thāoying Mō) was revered locally as a powerful spirit, the monument re-positioned her as a heroine of the Thai nation. The building of this monument so soon after the Bovaradej rebellion has been interpreted as an act to ensure the loyalty of northeastern people (Saipin Kaewngarmprasert 1995; also see Keyes 2002).[4]

After the Bovaradej rebellion was successfully put down, King Prajadhipok left the country for exile in the United Kingdom. When he died in 1935, the government engineered the choice of his nephew, Ananda Mahidol, to be king. Because King Ananda was a minor and continued to live in Switzerland where he was studying, the country was without an active monarch until after World War II.

More research also needs to be done on what reactions northeastern villagers had to the absence of a monarch whose Buddhist charisma (*bārāmī*) might have been seen as a source of power. What is known is that villagers responded very positively to the opportunity to elect representatives (*phūthāen*) to provincial and national assemblies (Keyes 1967; Dārārat Mēttārikānon 2003). In a real sense, during the 1930s villagers turned to *phūthāen* instead of *phūmībun* as those who could wield power for their benefit.

Representative democracy would not, however, prove to be a lasting resolution to the crisis of power that began with the coup of 1932. By 1938, Field Marshal Phibun Songgram succeeded in assuming pre-eminence among the 'Promoters' and adopted a pro-Japanese style fascism with himself as 'leader' (*prathān*). There is clear evidence (Keyes 1967; Dārārat Mēttārikānon 2003) that Phibun's ultranationalism did not become hegemonic for Northeasterners. On the contrary, after Phibun allied Thailand with Japan, Northeasterners gave significant support to the pro-Allies Free Thai movement.

The resignation of Phibun in 1944 and the defeat of Japan in 1945 seemed to open the way for the restoration of parliamentary democracy in Thailand. However, the governments of the immediate postwar period, led by Pridi Phanomyong and other Free Thai leaders, were undermined by economic problems and, most of all, by the death of King Ananda.

The 'Northeastern Problem' and the return of the monarchy

After Phibun returned to power in 1947, he and General Phao – the head of the police and Minister of Interior – moved to suppress the leading politicians of the Northeast who were deemed to be supporters of Pridi. In 1949 three leading MPs from the Northeast were arrested and then killed 'while trying to escape.' In 1952 another leading northeastern MP was assassinated. The ostensible reason for these extrajudicial murders and for other repression of politicians from the Northeast was that they were proponents of separating the Northeast from Thailand and joining it to Laos. In fact, as Dārārat and I have documented (Dārārat Mēttārikānon 2003; Keyes 1967), the real reason was that these politicians sought to promote policies that addressed the conditions of northeastern people. These policies were actually threatening because they were populist and thus represented a challenge to the control of power by security forces. Northeastern MPs were acutely aware of the poverty endemic in the region and the growing disparity between the northeastern agriculturally based economy and the national economy, which was growing in part because the rice premium (essentially a farm gate tax) was being used to fund investments in Bangkok and the central region.

In 1957 Field Marshal Sarit Thanarat, who had headed the army under Phibun, broke with him and General Phao and took power in a coup. After doing so, Sarit presented himself as a Northeasterner, as he had been born of an Isan mother in Mukdahan, although his father was in fact a Central Thai military officer. Sarit began to promote policies designed to help address what had come to be termed the 'Northeastern Problem' (*panhā Īsān*). This problem was construed to be manifest in political dissent that could lead to separatism but, in contrast to the Phibun government, the problem was also seen as rooted in the economic conditions of the region.

Sarit and his government decided to adopt a development programme specifically designed for the Northeast as part of the first National Development Plan in 1961 (Thailand. *Khanakammakan phatthana tawanôkchiang nüa* 1961 and Thailand. The Committee on Development of the Northeast n.d. [1961]). When this plan began to be implemented in 1962-63, there was initially a positive reception in the Northeast. This was made apparent to my wife and I when we were undertaking fieldwork in a village in Mahasarakham at this time. When Sarit died in December 1963, many villagers told us that the government would now no longer take an interest in the Northeast since his successor, Field Marshal Thanom Kittikachorn, was not a Northeasterner. That Sarit was a dictator was also acceptable to many Northeasterners because he was recognisable as a macho type well known to them as a *nakleng*. Thak Chaloemtiarana, in his study of Sarit, has characterised the *nakleng* as: 'a person who is not afraid to take risks, a person who "lives dangerously", kind to his friends but cruel to his enemies, a compassionate person, a gambler, a heavy drinker, and a lady-killer' (1979: 339).

Although the ideal male as understood in northeastern Thai culture is a man who has tempered his desires by having served a period as a Buddhist monk, the *nakleng* still inspires admiration as well as fear. In a real sense, Sarit was acceptable to northeastern villagers because he used his *nakleng* status to promote a paternalistic concern for the problems of the Northeast.

The Sarit era, however, was much more significant because it was associated with the restoration of the monarchy. The young King Bhumipol had returned to Thailand in the early 1950s: 'In 1955, the king made a ceremonial progression through the northeastern region of the country and was enthusiastically welcomed by the people' (Wilson 1962: 114). Phibun, who had always been deeply skeptical of the monarchy, was not pleased and disallowed any more government funding for the king's travels within the country. Sarit, by contrast, saw the monarchy as the source of legitimacy which he lacked, not having been one of the Promoters of the 1932 coup (Thak 1979: 311).

Despite his own personal relationship with the Northeast, Sarit was aware of the widespread disaffection of Northeasterners that had grown since Phibun had returned to power. The 'Northeastern Problem' had become more worrisome because representatives of the Communist Party of Thailand had begun to capitalise on this disaffection in seeking the support of villagers. With the Communist-led Pathet Lao in Laos holding half of that country, the fear of separatism was now linked by the Sarit government to the fear of communist revolution. The King was recruited to deploy his charisma in persuading Northeasterners to resist both separatism and communism.

In August 1962, the king addressed a meeting of commune and village leaders from the Northeast to warn them against adverse propaganda and subversion. He urged them to think about national unity and integration and told them: '*Being Thai does not necessarily depend on the religion one follows nor the customs and language used. There may be variations, but we are all Thai. We follow the same flag and share common aspirations.*' (quoted in Thak 1979: 318; original emphasis).

Villagers clearly were impressed by the visits of King Bhumipol, and his role led to the development of a new culture of power among northeastern villagers. He was seen unequivocally as possessing *bārāmī*, or in northeastern terms, he was a *phūmībun*. At the same time, they recognised that those who exercised power in his name – the bureaucrats known as *khārātchakān*, 'servants of the king' – and especially the military (*thahān*) were not their own chosen representatives. What northeastern villagers in the 1960s came to hope for was a political order headed by the King in which their own representatives (*phūthāēn*) would have a significant voice in shaping policies affecting their own quotidian lives.

The upheavals of the student-led overthrow of the dictatorship in 1973 and the counter-coup that restored the military to power in 1976 were viewed by villagers as events of the capital. Meanwhile, the Communist Party succeeded in attracting a growing following among northeastern villagers who had strong grievances against Bangkok-appointed bureaucrats and Thai military forces. The Party, however, never understood the attachment of villagers to the King nor the roots of their political culture in Buddhism.[5]

Development of populist democracy

Beginning in the 1980s there was a marked change in Thai politics that created a space for Northeasterners to begin again to have a political voice again through their elected representatives. A faction of the military whose leaders – especially Generals Kriangsak Chamanand, Prem Tinsalanond and Chawalit Yongchaiyut – had long experience in trying to win the 'hearts and minds' of northeastern villagers in combating the communist insurgency, saw a role for an elected parliament. At the same time, the new economic elite of the country began to see parliamentary democracy as a means to force the military and bureaucracy to share power with them. From the 1980s on, many candidates for parliament as well as workers for political parties received substantial financial support to ensure election of candidates favourable to their interests. Other factions of the military, in alliance with some senior members of the bureaucracy and royalist elite, resisted these developments and in 1991 and again in 2006 staged successful coups to restore their dominance of the political system. These coups notwithstanding, by the mid-1980s the principle that power in the name of the King should be exercised by an elected parliament became firmly established.

Northeastern villagers have felt increasing empowerment under parliamentary democracy because their votes constitute nearly a third of the electorate. This became especially true after the advent of Thaksin Shinawatra and the Thai Rak Thai Party. Although some politicians and parties in previous elections had sought the support of Northeasterners – former Prime Minister Chatichai Choonhavan had made Khorat in the Northeast the base of his own personal parliamentary support and General Chawalit Yongchaiyut campaigned by identifying with the Northeast – none succeeded in gaining the support that Thaksin and Thai Rak Thai did.

In 2005 my wife Jane and I were engaged in a restudy of Ban Nông Tün, the village in Mahasarakham province where we had first carried out fieldwork in the early 1960s. We were there in February 2005 when a national election resulted in the landslide victory for Thai Rak Thai. The almost total sweep of seats in the Northeast clearly demonstrated that this region was a primary base for Thaksin.

Many critics of Thaksin have suggested that he 'bought' this and previous elections. While the TRT was certainly well-financed and candidates for TRT were able to make their presence better known in the region than were the candidates of any other party, our own interviews with voters in Ban Nông Tün demonstrated that they enthusiastically supported Thaksin because of his populist policies – the 30-baht health scheme, the million baht fund for loans in each village, real devolution of power and taxing authority to Tambon Administrative Organisations being the most prominent. Several people we interviewed told us that, to paraphrase, in the past, politics was always controlled by people in Bangkok; today they could see that their votes had helped elect a government.

Since the early 1960s an increasing percentage of villagers from the Northeast work for extended periods away from the village, mostly in the Greater Bangkok Metropolitan Region. The urban workforce in Bangkok is overwhelmingly made up of Northeasterners. Most of these workers identify themselves as 'villagers' (*chāo bān*) rather than as urban workers. And because they travel back and forth to their home communities and join with other 'villagers' in Bangkok in attending events where Isan music (notably *môlam*) and Isan comedians perform, they remain deeply rooted in the cultural traditions of the Northeast. They share the same culture of power with those who still live in the villages – a culture of power that, as I have tried to describe here, is significantly different to that of the Bangkok elites.[6]

The coup that occurred in September 2006 has been interpreted by a number of analysts as rooted in an effort on the part of the old military/bureaucratic/royalist elite to re-assert its authority against those who would rule the country through buying votes and corruption. Since the King has been clearly linked in a variety of symbolic ways to the coup group, it has puzzled many as to why Northeasterners can continue to see the King as the charismatic source of political legitimacy and yet reject those who wield power in his name. That this was the case was evident in the overwhelming rejection by Northeasterners of the new constitution. I would note that the rejection was probably much greater than the actual numbers showed because it was so difficult in that election for those living in Bangkok and elsewhere outside the region to return to their home villages to vote.

There is, however, no contradiction in the minds of Northeasterners. The failure of the *phūmībun* uprising in the early part of the 20th century effectively ended efforts by local charismatic figures to challenge the authority of the King of Siam/Thailand. And since the restoration of the monarchy in the 1950s, Northeasterners have demonstrated that they widely revere King Bhumipol as the ultimate source of legitimation. At the same time, they have also long come to understand that those who actually exercise power in the King's name may do so against the best interests of Northeasterners. The representatives they have supported are seen as men who are loyal to the King, but who will also give voice to the concerns of the 'people', meaning the *chāo bān* of Isan. It is this continuity of a distinctive ethnoregionalism in northeastern Thailand that shows the limits of 'ideological domination' for those who would seek to join autocratic rule with royal legitimacy.

Epilogue

Throughout 2008 and early 2009, the difference in political culture between those who have sought to perpetuate (or, perhaps, re-establish) a 'guided' democracy predicated on royal legitimation and those who seek

to ensure that the moves towards a popular democracy that began during the governments of Prime Minister Thaksin Shinawatra continue
became much more pronounced. The roots of the confrontation between the proponents of these different visions of political order can be
traced to protests against Thaksin that began in late 2005.

These protests were organised by the People's Alliance for Democracy (PAD) led by Sondhi Limthongkul, a media magnate, and General
Chamlong Srimuang, a former mayor of Bangkok and leader of a now
defunct political party. Both had been erstwhile supporters of Thaksin.
PAD gained wide support not only from among the urban middle class
but also from many academics and activists working with non-govern-
mental organisations who were upset by Thaksin's extra-legal repression of drug dealers, his authoritarian prosecution of the war against in-
surrectionists in the Malay-speaking Muslim area of southern Thailand,
and his use of power to enrich his family and cronies. PAD also received support from high-ranking Privy Councillors and military and
bureaucratic officials with strong links to the palace whom McCargo
has characterised as forming a 'network monarchy' (2005).

The protests organised by PAD coupled with a court decision that in-
validated a snap election Thaksin had called in April 2006 led to a political stalemate that was seemingly ended by a coup in September 2006.
General Sonthi Boonyaratglin, the commander-in-chief of the army who
led the coup, and General Surayud Chulanont, whom the junta chose to
lead an interim government, promised that political order would be restored and elections held under a new constitution.

From September 2006 until December 2007, the Surayud government backed by the junta sought to ensure – through the constitution-
drafting process and the strengthening of conservative judicial institutions – that new elections would lead to the formation of a government
that excluded Thaksin and his allies and was led, instead, by 'good
men'. In December 2007, elections were held for the first time since
the coup of 2006. Under acts promulgated under the government in-
stalled by the coup leaders and the new constitution, the Thai Rak Thai
Party had been banned and most of its leaders not allowed to stand for
political office. Despite these strong constraints, a successor party to the
Thai Rak Thai and its allies still won a majority of seats in Parliament.
The Democrat Party, led by Abhisit Vejjajiva with backing from the
royalist-military elite and strong support from the urban middle class,
became the opposition in Parliament.

The governments formed during 2008 were crippled and ultimately
brought down not by a new election in which the Democrats gained a
majority but by a series of legal actions that led to the resignation of
one prime minister, the banning of more members of parliament associated with the successor parties to the Thai Rak Thai, and by the inepti-

tude of a number of government ministers. Most of all, political change was a consequence of intensifying street demonstrations organised by a resurgent PAD.

In December 2008, the PAD led its members, who had been occupying the prime minister's office and other government buildings for several months, to take over Bangkok's international airports. The military and police, although called on by the then government to restore order, failed to do so. When a Constitutional Court determined that the leaders of the successor party to the Thai Rak Thai were no longer eligible to serve in parliament, and when a faction of this party defected, the Democrat Party was able to gain sufficient parliamentary support to form a new government.

A movement known as the National United Front of Democracy against Dictatorship (UDD) whose support was overwhelmingly drawn from rural Northeasterners and their urban working class kinsmen, began protests against the Abhisit government. Whereas the followers of the PAD had worn yellow shirts to demonstrate their loyalty to the King, whose birthday colour is yellow, the followers of the UDD donned red shirts. Although why red had been chosen as the colour for their movement is somewhat unclear, it is widely seen in Thailand as a colour associated with revolution.

At the time of the traditional Thai New Year (Songkran) in April 2009, there were very large Red Shirt demonstrations in Bangkok and in the eastern resort town of Pattaya. These demonstrations culminated with the Red Shirts taking over the streets of Bangkok and forcing the cancellation of an Asian summit that brought together the leaders of the ten-member Association of Southeast Asian Nations (ASEAN) together with the leaders of China, Japan, South Korea, India, Australia and New Zealand. That the Red Shirts could accomplish this at a hotel on a bluff in Pattaya stunned the government and even many sympathisers. The movement had, however, become a mob, with many members no longer following their leaders. Like their ancestors who had joined the *phūmībun* uprising a century earlier, their strong belief in their righteous cause was no match for the military force that was belatedly deployed against them.

As of late 2009, the significance of the events of Songkran 2009 was still being vigorously debated. While the PAD interprets the Red Shirt movement as having been recruited with money provided by the very wealthy Thaksin, and advocates strong punishment for the leaders of the movement, it seems clear that the Red Shirt movement is far from being the creation solely of a politician who often used power for personal gain rather than for the benefit of the country or even his supporters. Rather, the mass support for the movement, like the large electoral majorities for the Thai Rak Thai and successor parties, indicates that

Northeasterners are not willing to give up the significant political influence they gained during the Thaksin period and to return to being 'happy peasants'. To the contrary, they seek to have their own political culture given greater recognition and respect than it had been under previous governments or would be under a government acceptable to the PAD and others who favor a version of guided democracy.

Notes

1   There were other uprisings during the period from the late 1890s through the first decade of the 20th century (see Tej Bunnag 1968; also in Tej Bunnag 1981; Tanabe 1984; Wilson 1997). The ones in the Northeast were, however, much larger (Tej Bunnag 1967; also in Tej Bunnag 1981; Ishii 1975; Murdoch 1975; Keyes 1977; Chatthip Nartsupha 1984; Wilson 1997).

2   *Kamma* is the Pali-language version of the Sanskrit-derived Karma. Pali is the language used for Buddhist texts in Thailand. [Eds.]

3   These designations were used in documents written by officials at the time. I have given the full references to these documents in previous publications (Keyes 1973, 1977).

4   The term 'rebelliousness' appears in a flyer circulated in Khorat in 1996 when Saipin's book became a source of controversy (see Keyes 2002: 113)

5   I have provided the detailed basis for this conclusion in a forthcoming paper (Keyes, forthcoming).

6   Pattana Kittiarsa (2001, 2005, 2006, 2009a, 2009b, 2009c) has written the most incisive analyses of how Isan popular culture in its more modern guises shapes the identities of Northeasterners.

2 Transforming Agrarian Transformation in a Globalizing Thailand

Anan Ganjanapan and Philip Hirsch

In a country whose countryside has changed so fundamentally since the 1970s, what is the continuing relevance and significance of frameworks, empirical investigations and analyses of agrarian transformation from the previous era? In this chapter, we consider changes in the study of rural change, looking at new contexts of study and new conceptual lenses through which we now view social and agricultural relations and their change in the Thai countryside. We also reflect specifically on Andrew Turton's contribution to questions of power and contestation in the agrarian change literature of the time he was writing, and its legacy for the current scholarship on agrarian transformation. We try to contextualise Turton's work within the times he was writing, draw attention to some of the changes that have taken place since then and to approach some of the themes his work raises in a new light.

Agrarian transformation in Southeast Asia, and in Thailand in particular, is a key theme of Turton's anthropological writings during the 1970s and 1980s. His concern for rural social justice is also an important part of his reputation as an activist scholar. Beginning with his PhD thesis in 1976 and extending to various essays in his seminal co-edited book on agrarian transformation of 1989, his works made an important contribution to our understanding of agrarian changes, to the contemporary situation of the Thai countryside, and to ways in which to understand power and its (ab)uses in governing rural social relations.

Turton's co-edited collection with Hart, White and others was part of a project that set out to do two things: '... to integrate and compare evidence on the rapid and profound agrarian changes taking place in different countries in [Southeast Asia], and to address the conceptual and methodological problems involved in understanding these changes' (1989: xiii). The study of rural change during the period on which the book was based – the 1970s and 1980s – was thus specifically set within both the material conditions and the framing concepts of the time.

Empirically, there were some defining contexts for the *Agrarian Transformations* book, and it is to those contexts that we now turn. First and foremost, the cases chosen from four Southeast Asian countries including Thailand were deliberately focused on core rice-growing areas. Rice was taken as the heartland crop around which the mainstay of agrarian society was based. Second, the green revolution and its accompanying technological and social changes formed the backdrop to changes in production methods, labour relations, land ownership and tenancy, the role of capital and so on. Third, the increasing level of inequality in the countryside and between the countryside and the city was a generic phenomenon to be explained and critiqued.

Conceptually, *Agrarian Transformations* was shaped around the theme of rural differentiation; that is, the processes of class formation and sharpening of power difference in the countryside between different groups of rural producers and social actors. With this core and contested process in mind, the second key conceptual concern was linking local processes at the village level to wider political and economic currents, processes and structures. The role of the state and its relationship with capitalist-oriented economic development was a key to the analysis, which 'emphasise[d] the need to take explicit account of the power structures within which technological change and commercialization occur' (ibid. 2). This required a linking of the hitherto rather separate detailed village ethnographies by anthropologists, on the one hand, with wider political-economy framed analysis of state and class at the national level and with an emphasis on urban, industrial 'fractions' on the other.

More specifically on Thailand, about which Turton contributed two chapters in *Agrarian Transformations* – one national overview on the agrarian underpinnings of the Thai state, one on local powers – we see a state framed in the 1980s as having a power base contingent on a particular agrarian social formation. Turton represents the Thai state as a predatory one, in the sense that it had always taken much more out of the countryside than it had put back, in part through surpluses extracted from the smallholder-based rice economy. In turn, the state had progressively entrenched itself at a local level through 'local powers' to contain disquiet and unrest, and to give key gatekeepers a stake in the status quo. Thailand was represented at that time as a country that, despite accelerating industrialisation and diversification, remained a largely agricultural society at least in a demographic sense, and still heavily dependent on rice farming within the agricultural sector. Detailed discussion of the local power elite revealed them to have significant agricultural interests in land and other factors of production, but also pecuniary benefits from their position as interlocutors of state-led and financed development programmes, often through positions of formal local leadership as village heads and *kamnans*. Processes of incipient class formation were identified, for example in the notion of 'wage labour equivalence' among peasants who maintained formal ownership of small plots of land but lost autonomy over decisions on how to farm it.

However, it must be said that the Thai countryside has changed in a number of key respects in the three decades since the 1970s, and the lenses through which we look at such change have also been reshaped. A number of authors have addressed the empirical changes head-on. Jonathan Rigg's work on de-agrarianisation (2001) emphasises the declining role of agriculture in the portfolio of individual, household and village economic activities in favour of migration and remittances, service and manufacturing-based incomes. Hirsch (1994) identifies changes in the Thai countryside that challenge assumptions and stereotypes of rural life as agriculturally based and rice-dominated, of agrarian relations and social differentiation as geared mainly around land rather than other factors of production, of environmentalism as a preoccupation of a small educated urban elite rather than a concern relevant to livelihoods of the rural poor drawn into the wider sweep of development, of rural dissent as based mainly in core rice-growing areas rather than at a periphery where conflicts over forest and forest land shape the 'front line' of agrarian conflict, and of village communities as the social field within which most agrarian relations are played out. Agriculture, it should be pointed out, now employs less than half the country's workforce, and most of that minority draws significant parts of their income from outside the agricultural sector, while agriculture now accounts for less than 10 per cent of the total value of national economic production. Within the agricultural sector, enormous structural changes have taken place including agribusiness and vertical integration, while organic farming and associated influences of consumer preferences, sufficiency economy programmes and discourses, together with other new currents, frame the current context in which farming continues to change in complex ways. The implications of such radical changes for the study of rural change are enormous, and they do make the class-oriented political economic analysis of an earlier era more difficult to apply and less immediately resonant with understandings of the key issues in rural change than they were in that earlier era.

Some of the new lenses through which we look at agrarian change today reflect dominant issues and concerns that are closely related to Thailand's societal evolution and place in the world. For example, the emergence of environmentalism (Hirsch 1997) would have been difficult to envisage even as late as the 1980s, yet it fundamentally affects the conditions under which rural people farm, their access to land and other natural resources, their relationships with the state and state development projects and, increasingly, the markets for which they produce (Vandergeest 2008). Globalization and the ways in which it ties the Thai countryside into neoliberal currents is materialised through trade and vertically integrated production, but it is also discursively significant in the ways in which countryside values are shifted beyond the production of crops to recreation and other spheres of consumption.

Despite being shaped by its times, there is much in Turton's work that presaged some of these new directions in the study of agrarian transformation, and there is also much that influenced these directions. He specifically identifies a need for poststructuralist analysis to be brought into the study of power in class as well as non-class processes in rural Thai society. The discursive bent reflected in his 'Limits of Ideological Domination' (1984) and his framing of participation as an arena of contestation provided his students and others who took up the study of power in the Thai countryside with approaches that sat easily with the still embryonic 'post-development' approach at the time he was writing.

Turton's key insight into studies of agrarian transformation was, therefore, to invite us to turn our attention to the reality of social actors through their discursive practices of power as manifested in local processes and social relations. This invitation was conceptually an important turning point because it opened up a critical approach to agrarian studies with a strong emphasis on the *politics of transformation* itself (Turton 1989a).

Such an invitation was also methodologically significant because it suggested an escape from the mind-trap of a peasant-state dichotomy, which was an approach so dominantly subscribed to by most scholars at that time. Following this methodological guideline allowed for an early interest in the complexity as well as dynamism of rural processes as the *study of the in-between.*

To guide us into this line of research, Turton introduced various ways of operationalising his study of the in-between space and processes, ways that have since become common practice. He began with an emphasis on power relations between key actors. Not focusing exclusively on the process of agrarian differentiation as seen at a village level, he also brought to our attention the powerful group of intermediaries which he called '*local powers*' who exercised their power in between the state and peasant at the so called local level (Turton 1989a; see also Cohen, this volume). These local powers were neither an integral part of the state, nor could they simply be considered as villagers. Instead, they manipulated their power through maintaining their close connection with both the state and market while dominating villagers through patronage relations.

What was most significant in his study of complex power relations is that Turton managed to go beyond a unitary level of analysis by focusing on the *multiplicity of power relations*. In addition to the materiality in political-economic levels of power relations, his major contribution was in the analysis of *ideological domination*, which he managed to argue convincingly was a key part of the exercise of power, yet was limited in practice (1984). Underlying such limitation is the subject matter of what Turton had long researched and revealed as one of the key contradictions in the process of agrarian transformation.

Most of Turton's works on agrarian transformation concentrated on the study of such contradictions within the in-between spaces of power relations that he characterized conceptually through his notion of *participation* (1987). These contradictions were understood not only in abstraction but also in practices as politics of negotiation, although Turton at that time had not yet used this specific word (see Rigg, this volume). Thus, in his works, he placed considerable importance on these contradictions as politics of participation that were manifested in several forms of struggle as found in the mixture of social movements and individualistic resistance in everyday life, both in ideological space as well as in the socio-political sphere.

In short, the analysis of ideological limits of domination appears to be Turton's most significant contribution to the understanding of the politics of agrarian transformation. Superficially, one might find such analysis today encountering its own limits, since many of the contextual underpinnings of the analysis are, it is true, specific mainly to the context of those two decades (the 1970s and 1980s), relating mainly to land-based agricultural production and state ideology. The agrarian transformation spoken of then was more or less about market integration of the peasant economy, mainly in the area of commodity markets with limited opportunities in off-farm labour markets.

But processes of agrarian transformation of the subsequent two decades have changed greatly in terms of content. It can be considered that agrarian transformation itself is transforming in the context of a globalizing economy of neoliberalism. The clearest manifestation of this is that rural societies themselves have been rapidly restructured. They can no longer rely mainly on land-based agricultural production under the state and market control, of the type considered by Turton, but depend more on capital-based production and labour markets with complex connections to the global market and regionalisation of development.

These changes notwithstanding, Turton's approaches, as highlighted above, continue to be conceptually relevant to the study of current processes of agrarian transformation, even within the context of globalization. Globalization during the past two decades has increasingly become a major force for rapid structural changes in contemporary rural Southeast Asia and Thailand in particular. Its effect may even be characterised as another 'great rural transformation' in Polanyian terminology (Polanyi 1957). But rather than being embedded in the social structure, as Polanyi tried to argue, the current transformation has an ability to transform the agrarian transformation itself, in a form of rural restructuring. This ongoing rural restructuring is clearly manifested in at least three overlapping areas, and here we consider the themes raised by Turton in a more contemporary context.

Natural resources are the most basic area of rural restructuring, where so-called 'market-based land reform' is actively carried out by most Southeast Asian governments. The privatisation of property or the commoditisation of land is the most common strategy. The rapid expansion of commercial plantations, notably rubber trees, is an important example. Another strategy is the capitalisation of resources that can be frequently seen in the form of dam constructions for generating electrical power. The unintended consequences of these changes on the one hand intensify resource competition between various actors, both within and outside the rural sector, who have competing or conflicting uses for those resources. On the other hand, they reinforce livelihood insecurity for the marginal groups, notably ethnic minorities living in upland areas (Hirsch & Wyatt 2004).

The second new area of rural restructuring can be found in the flexible and diversified employment of labour, where agriculture is being displaced by sub-contracted manufacturing, small-scale industry and local tourism. Together with industrial expansion into rural areas, the rural sector is increasingly being integrated into the global market without a clear mechanism for negotiation. At the same time, the rural environment becomes more and more polluted. Not only faced with insecure livelihoods, rural labourers become even more invisible in the eyes of the state welfare systems that treat them merely as informal workers.

The last area of recent rural restructuring occurs at the regional level across national borders in the name of regionalisation of development, particularly in the Greater Mekong Subregion (GMS). Here, market-driven mechanisms are working at bridging rural interconnectedness through various networks of highways, cross-border trade, and tourism, as well as power and water grids. These regional connections not only encourage greater resource mobilisation but also spread epidemic diseases through cross-border labour migrations and other forms of population movements. Under the borderless situation, contradictions often result. Although Southeast Asian rural people's lives are being brought into closer proximity with one another than in the past decade, many of them have become even further excluded from their access to both natural resources and secure livelihoods (Hirsch 2001) in ways that earlier analyses could not have foreseen.

In this sense, the ongoing rural restructuring in Southeast Asia can be seen more as a contradictory process than a golden road to modernity because of its many unintended consequences. Underlying such transformation is the intensification of the competition for control over common natural resources. In fact, it can be considered more as a 'politics of exclusion' because of the marginalisation of livelihoods of the majority of the rural population whose life has become increasingly insecure and fraught with environmental risk.

However, most studies on the relationship between globalization and rural society tend to be one-sided by emphasising mainly the powerful forces of globalization on restructuring rural economies, especially those grounded in regulation theory. Alternatively, other approaches have focused more on local enclosures of globalization or the global embeddedness in locality (Korff 2003). It is only recently that some scholars have begun to call our attention to the politics of globalization, along quite a similar line of argument to Turton's politics of agrarian transformation a few decades earlier. They argue that 'the impact of globalization on rural localities is revealed not as domination or subordination but as negotiation, manipulation and hybridization, conducted through but not contained by local micro-politics' (Woods 2007: 487).

Although politics have increasingly been perceived as a critical dimension in the globalization process, most studies conceptually remain focused mainly on the level of the socio-political sphere. In his studies of the politics of agrarian transformation, however, Turton tried not to limit himself only to that particular level but strongly engaged in the multiplicity or dialectic of power relations by taking the politics of ideology and knowledge as practices in forms of resistance. This was clearly seen in his analysis of 'invulnerability' as an important concept in northern Thai local knowledge that is both discourse and practice of resistance at the same time (1991a). Such conceptualisation also remains crucial to the study of the current politics of globalization and rural restructuring with a focus on differentiated social actors.

The outstanding problem with this kind of conceptualisation, however, is that local knowledge often seems to be primarily understood as given or existing by itself. Even though it can be reproduced in the context of conflicting power relations, such an approach seems somewhat limited in its understanding of generative and practical complexities of knowledge. Here, some kind of reconceptualising of knowledge may be required. It could begin firstly by following Turton's conceptualization of knowledge as both discourse and practice. However, instead of taking the existing forms of knowledge that are more essentialistic in nature, it might alternatively be reconceptualised through the concept of '*knowledge space*'.

The concept of 'knowledge space' was first introduced in mathematical psychology by Doignon and Falmagne in 1985 as a combinatorial structure describing the possible states of knowledge of a human learner (1985). In 1994, Pierre Levy, Professor of Hypermedia at the University of Paris, applied the concept to cyberspace and digital communications (1997). But it was not until 1997 that David Turnbull gave the concept its socio-cultural dimension (1997: 553). He began by recognising that knowledge production is a social activity as well as a social history of space. It involves contingent processes of making assemblages and linkages, of creating spaces in which knowledge is possible. The emphasis on this spatial dimension of knowledge opens up the possibility of seeing knowledge more clearly as practices by knowledge producers. These practices, especially through social strategies of negotiation, allow knowledge producers to create spaces that can generate new forms of knowledge from heterogeneous and isolated knowledges.

Based initially on Turnbull, the concept of 'knowledge space' is further conceptualised as forming places of both knowledge and power production in the sense that they are contested spaces associated with complex social relations. Following this conceptualisation, knowledge spaces can be seen to represent the very regimes through which truth, knowledge and powers are created (Wright 2005: 904). In contrast to situated forms of knowledge, or 'negotiating' forms of knowledge, which are only conceived as generating knowledge in a particular context of contestation (Nygren 1999; Pottier et al. eds. 2003), knowledge space is considered as *a third space of practice* which also creates that context.

The concept of 'knowledge space' may go somewhat beyond Turton's idea of knowledge in terms of its dynamism and multiplicity. However, it still concurs with his strong interest in the politics of knowledge as well as the study of the in-between. In this sense, the notion of 'knowledge space' helps to bridge the spheres of power and knowledge, or the politico-economic sphere as well as ideological space, through a third space of practice that implies a politics of knowledge as resistance in a multiplicity of spaces and as a practice of changing power relations. Thus, it seems to provide a meaningful framework for the contemporary analysis of agrarian transformation in the current context of globalization because so many key actors are shifting their spaces of struggle in more complex ways than hitherto.

Under globalization today, agrarian transformation is not only about rural restructuring in the socio-economic sphere, but also about the changing politics of increasingly contested forms of knowledge. In addition to market-oriented ways of thinking, most so-called development programmes are carried out in the name of scientific knowledge. But such claims of scientific knowledge involve a strong degree of shifting justification. In many cases, for example, the state highland development programmes which claim to be a strategy to civilize the margins in fact are merely an excuse to exclude upland ethnic minority groups from their resources (Duncan 2004).

Sometimes, this type of transformation in development can be clearly seen as expressing a politics of conservation. In the case of the policy of eliminating shifting cultivation in favour of sedentary agriculture, swidden agriculture – which is often a form of agroforestry – is generically stigmatised as a kind of forest destruction that flies in the face of applying modern knowledge of science in agriculture. In this sense, state conservation policy can simply be considered a myth because it is only strictly enforced on the marginal ethnic groups while at the same time allowing for greater expansion of plantations at the expense of forest and shifting fields. Underlying such a politics of conservation, then, is actually an intensive competition for resources by various actors who use different kinds of knowledge to justify their claims and policies (Anan 1997), and it is important to recognise this in the current situation.

The current processes of agrarian transformation and rural restructuring in Southeast Asia are in fact dominated by such contesting forms of knowledge. Under these contradictions and conflicting relationships, differentiated actors in rural communities do not merely remain passive. On the contrary, they are actively engaging through their everyday life in what can be considered as 'negotiating livelihoods' within 'knowledge spaces' where development strategies can be locally initiated and can contest mainstream practice.

In the case of highland communities, a knowledge space can be initiated in the process of negotiating livelihoods around practices such as shifting cultivation. By diversifying their shifting farming patterns, some communities can adopt biological diversity as their adaptive strategy under pressures of relocation by the state. Others may choose to frame their practices by employing the terminology and dynamics of agroforestry as a practice of negotiation with state policy, which tends to favour commercial plantations.

After a long engagement in the struggle for their negotiated livelihood, several villages may also join together in performing rituals in a way that embodies another form of their knowledge space, such as the rituals of forest ordination that are currently performed both as contesting and negotiating practices in the discourses of conservation (Isager & Ivarsson 2002). These rituals are not only spaces for identity construction but, as a type of new knowledge space, they also allow for the participation of a wide diversity of actors with multiple interests, such as NGOs, officials and academics. They also create a context for the kind of learning process and network that is so essential for generating new forms of knowledge, especially the complex knowledge of rights, power and governance in negotiation through debate.

These engagements are not always carried out in isolation but, in several cases, ethnic minority communities have been able to form ethnically based knowledge networks as a 'knowledge space' in which their contesting identities can be expressed. Some such networks can also be further developed into social movements, such as in the case of the campaign for community forest law in Thailand.

Many rural communities are also engaging their knowledge spaces as practices of learning processes through the so-called 'people's research' (in Thai, *Thai Ban* research) in order to contest and negotiate with the domination of scientific knowledge. For some peri-urban areas where industrial pollution has become a major problem of environmental risk, community-driven regulations occasionally have taken over from state law enforcement. Such practices can also be seen as new knowledge spaces where a particular form of governance can be generated.

In this sense, the new knowledge spaces that are formed not only allow for negotiating livelihoods but also help in engaging rural actors more and more in participatory development and shifting spaces of struggle. This kind of participation has given rural actors a crucial role in transforming the transformation that tends to be based only on certain knowledges within neoliberal ideology. The emerging transformation can be seen in some kinds of alternative livelihoods and modes of governance, albeit ones that are often only emerging in a few specific areas.

In conclusion, the various forms of rural actors' political engagement in the knowledge spaces that have been carved out can, in the context of globalization, encourage the formation of alternative systems of governance. These new kinds of governance, both at the national and international levels, enlarge the social drivers that regulate rural restructuring beyond those of only market-driven or state regulating mechanisms as conventionally understood. As a result, agrarian transformation itself continues to be transformed not just by global processes but also by differential social actors who are engaged in the politics of transformation. At one level, these politics and modes of governance are a long way from the radical class-based agrarian politics of a generation ago. At another level, Turton's early forays into discursive struggles, powerful elites articulating local and wider processes, and contestation based on cultural practices and recognition of the limits to domination can all be seen to resonate in the new nature and understanding we have of Thailand's agrarian transformation today.

3   Local Leaders and the State in Thailand

Paul T. Cohen

Andrew Turton's analysis of local leaders in Thailand is best viewed in terms of his attempt to unravel the relationship between violence and consent in relation to state power, and the limits of that power, drawing on a diverse range of theorists (poststructuralist, neo-Gramscian and neo-Marxist). In this paper I outline and evaluate Turton's writings on local leaders and the state in Thailand. I also endeavour to trace the relevance and connections of his work to earlier, contemporaneous and more recent scholarship relating to local headmen, dissident peasant leaders, provincial bosses, Village Scouts, urban gang leaders and charismatic Buddhist monks.

'Local powers'

Turton's key argument in several papers published in the 1980s is that ruling power is not maintained through 'morally persuasive' hegemonic leadership (in the Gramscian sense) based on the shared values of all classes of Thai but rather through ideological and violently coercive forms of domination. Turton sets himself the task of elucidating precisely the *connections between* ideological and (violently) repressive institutions. In doing so, he does not restrict his analysis to ideological or repressive *state institutions*. Rather he focuses on non-state local manifestations of power (which he refers to variously as 'local power structures' or 'local powers') and which constitute a 'secondary complex of predatory interests' (1984: 30).

According to Turton, these 'local powers' in the 1970s and early 1980s comprised a small minority (perhaps 5 per cent) in rural villages: large landowners, commodity dealers, shopkeepers, village officials, rice millers and money lenders. They gained advantages from external connections and alliances in linking the mass of villagers to state and market structures and in their ability to accumulate village surplus through rent, wages, retail prices, commodity dealing and interest (1984: 30; 1989a: 82). They maintained their dominance in village society through their controlling position as members of village committees and through personal patronage. Increasingly these 'community leaders' (*phunam chum-*

chon) were referred to by the village poor as *klum itthiphon* (influence groups) who had established themselves as a separate, cohesive 'society' (*sangkhom*) from which the poor felt excluded (Turton 1984: 31).

A key member of these 'local powers' was the *kamnan* (sub-district headman). The *kamnan*'s position of power and wealth was considerably enhanced in the mid-1970s with the establishment of the Tambon (sub-district) Development Fund as a potential source of graft. Also, the *kamnan* became a crucial link between the village 'upper stratum' and outsiders with political and commercial interests in villages, a link which he could exploit to his and their own advantage but often at the expense of the rural poor. This role of the *kamnan* reflects the radical changes in village political leadership.

Based on fieldwork from 1959 to 1961, Michael Moerman characterised the village headman as a synaptic leader. He provided a key link between state officials and rural villagers but, despite the conflicting demands of villagers and state officials, he generally worked to protect villagers against state exactions. 'His rewards of exercising power, skimming wealth, disseminating knowledge, and receiving respect all stem from his appearing to lead a strong community which he protects from powerful outsiders whose interests his villagers think are opposed to theirs' (Moerman 1969: 546). Turton, in one of his early papers that focused on his own fieldwork in Chiang Rai province, acknowledges the existence of this type of headman for the period 1950-1970: 'Villagers are making increasing use of headmen – as arbitrator, as middleman agent to deal with the bureaucracy, and as defender of community interests' (1976a: 283). However, he notes the emergence towards the end of the period of a 'second type of headman' who is 'more assiduous in his search for powerful economic and political patronage, and cultivates senior officials and urban traders whose interests are further removed from those of the headman's village constituency' (ibid. 284). Thus, the situation was 'one of considerable variation and change' and the relationship between headmen and fellow villagers had become 'increasingly contradictory' (ibid. 276). However, by the mid-1970s this contradiction had come closer to resolution as the headmen increasingly and consistently aligned their interests to those of the village 'upper stratum' and to the state. The *kamnan* was by then the 'eyes and ears' of the District Office (Turton 1984: 31). The *kamnan* and other members of the village 'upper stratum' were also strategically connected at the district level (in part due to their better education and knowledge of Central Thai) to large-scale landowners and merchants, millers and contractors and transport owners who often served as their patrons or even 'godfathers' (*chao pho*) (ibid. 32).

These mafia-type *chao pho* emerged in the 1970s with the growth of provincial capitalism but the heyday of these provincial businessmen and their influence on national politics was between the mid-1980s to mid-1990s. Their political power reached its apogee under the administration of Banharn Silpa-archa (1995-1996) – the first provincial boss to achieve national leadership. During this decade, after the publication of Turton's initial paper on 'local powers' (1989a), the phenomenon of *chao pho* attracted considerable media attention and also scholarly analysis (in particular, in Ruth McVey's edited volume *Money and Power in Provincial Thailand*, 2000). It is worth noting that, according to Pasuk and Baker (2004), the Thaksin Shinawatra government (2001-2006) launched an attack on the 'dark influences' of these provincial bosses as a means to remove competition to corporate business and Thaksin's political party.

'Local power structures' provide the main milieu for what Turton refers to as 'restrictive ideological practices'. His analysis of these practices reflects the influence of Foucault's study of the 'political technology of the body' and the 'micro-physics of power' (and the way power operates in a 'capillary' or net-like fashion from below) (Turton 1984: 38; 1986: 39, 41). It is from this perspective that Turton explores in depth the *connections* between ideological and violently coercive (repressive) forms. He singles out one extreme form of restrictive ideological practice that was common in the 1970s, namely the labelling, accusations and surveillance of virtually anyone who criticised local leaders or the government as 'communist' (1984: 50-56). This was a form of excommunication that had its traditional expression in practices such as accusing people of being a witch (*phi ka*), with the potential for these accusations to be used by wealthy villagers to target the poor (see Anan 1984).

A more recent example of restrictive ideological practice that culminated in violence is Thaksin's 'war on drugs' in 2003 in which drug dealers became the new external/internal 'Other' that threatened the 'geo-body' of the Thai nation. Thaksin likened methamphetamines (*ya ba*) to a cancer in the body politic, and the metaphor of disease from the communist era re-emerged in the context of the drug war. This provided the discursive climate for dehumanising drug dealers and the extrajudicial killings of them during the three-month war.

The process of labelling, accusation, surveillance, intimidation and dehumanisation of subjects as 'enemies of society' or 'enemies of the nation' serves to instil fear. Turton declares (quoting Therborn): 'Force and violence operate as a form of rule only through the ideological mechanism of *fear*' (1984: 60; original emphasis). Through the creation of a climate of fear, assent to the dominant discourse is increasingly 'demanded with menaces' (Turton quoting Gellner, 1984: 60; 1986: 43).

Turton also explicates the connection between ideology and (violent) coercion through the semantics of the word 'inculcation', which he translates as 'forcible teaching'. The word has the root meaning of stamping or impressing with the *heel* (Latin *calx*). The inculcation of nationalist and anti-communist ideology and its potential to culminate in violence is well demonstrated in his analysis of the Village Scout movement (*luk seua chao ban*). The movement was founded in 1971 by the Border Patrol Police and reached a peak in popularity in 1976. Turton notes: 'At the local level they are sponsored by officials of all kinds ... and local landowners, traders, bankers, and politicians – in other words the milieu of "local power structures" identified earlier' (1984: 53).

More than a decade later, Katherine Bowie explored the process of inculcation of this nationalist ideology in her anthropological study of the Village Scout movement in Sanpatong district, Chiang Mai. Loyalty to national symbols was most visibly instilled in villagers during initiation rituals that Bowie describes as a five-day 'psychological drama'. The rituals were so emotionally charged that they created a sense of euphoria and even hysteria among participants. The villagers' emotions reached a climax on the final day of the initiation when they were presented with royal kerchiefs that were blessed by the King and ascribed magical powers similar to that of Buddha images and amulets. Ritual symbolism did not only inculcate a strong sense of loyalty to Nation, Religion and King but also political unity against external enemies as well. 'The scout instructors were clearly trying to portray Thailand as a nation whose cultural survival was being threatened by external enemies who were infiltrating the country' (Bowie 1997: 191). This view was used to justify the extreme violence and atrocities inflicted by Village Scouts (along with Thai police and other right-wing groups) at Thammasat University on 6 October 1976 on students 'deceived' by communists, socialists or the Left.

The limits to state power: resistance

However, there are limits to ideological domination, as the title of Turton's 1984 paper signals: 'A fundamental, axiomatic limitation of ideological domination is the impossibility of total subjection' (1984: 62) – a point Turton reinforces by quoting Gellner that ideologies 'do not really have the conceptual power to make rival positions unthinkable' (ibid. 64). Resistance to dominant ideological discourse can be exposed in 'received or inherited popular culture'. This resistance may take the form of more individualistic 'everyday forms of resistance' or more collective and violent regional rebellions (such as the 1901-02 'Holy Men' uprising in the Northeast and the 1889 Panya Pap rebellion in the North). In another paper, Turton (1986) also identifies 'in-between' forms of resistance (or 'middle-range forms of struggle') such as new forms of autonomous peasant associations that emerged during the 1970s in Thailand (larger in scale than isolated acts of individual resistance and smaller than peasant uprisings) which develop 'new and transformed practices' (sharing information and experiences, travelling and visiting to extend links and alliances, new forms of knowledge and communication) – all of which encourage 'a new self-confidence and boldness' (1984: 66; 1986: 45)

In his analysis of the limits of ideological domination, Turton focuses on the discourse of invulnerability as a form of popular culture or local knowledge that serves to overcome or, at least, lessen fear by subordinate classes (1984: 61) and that has had an important place in 'everyday' forms of peasant resistance and in peasant rebellions (1991a: 156). This theme Turton explores in depth in a paper dedicated specifically to Northern Thai ideas and practices of invulnerability, based on his own fieldwork and work by other anthropologists working in the North, and which I consider to be arguably his finest piece of ethnographic writing.

The term commonly used in Northern Thailand for invulnerability is *kham* ('able to withstand'). A person becomes *kham* through possession and use of verbal formulae called *katha* which may be memorised, inscribed in the form of *yantra* or tattooed on the body (Turton 1991a: 161). *Kham* knowledge is used for individual protection in dangerous and frightening circumstances, especially in encounters with aggressive or malevolent humans (ibid. 159). Usually *kham* knowledge is acquired through a teacher (*khru*), and effective use is dependent on certain observances such as respect and offerings to 'spirit teachers' (*phi khru*), food taboos and appropriate forms of mental attitudes (such as meditation).

While Turton refers to *kham* knowledge as a form of 'local knowledge' or 'popular culture', he emphasises that such ideas traverse the elite/popular divide in what he calls a 'cross-hatching of discourses' (a term coined by Reynolds in the same volume). Thus the themes of *khongkraphan* ('invulnerable') and *khongkraphan chatri* ('invulnerable warrior') were common in Siamese court literature (Turton 1991a: 164-167) but also entered the popular discourse of invulnerability, indeed sometimes in a quite subversive way (ibid. 159; see also Cohen 1987).

Turton attests to the pervasiveness and importance of *kham* discourse in Northern Thailand (1991a: 163). Indeed he opines that 'It is virtually a requirement of leadership' (ibid. 170). In this respect he identifies a 'range of instances' whose reputation and power was linked with invulnerability ideas. He also asserts that invulnerability knowledge may be found in the context of 'competition for leadership or peer group pre-eminence' (ibid. 162). Implicit in his analysis is that this competition is most likely to be associated with younger, aggressive and intimidating men engaged in socially dubious activities, such as daredevil youths and various types of *nak leng* (tough guys or bandits). Pertinent here is

Anjalee Cohen's recent study of Chiang Mai gangs (*kaeng wai run*) that numbered as many as 70 in 2003. These urban youth gangs draw heavily on the enduring Northern Thai popular culture of masculinity that values fearlessness, courage, risk taking, capacity for violence, and invulnerability. With reference to Turton's paper on invulnerability and local knowledge, she describes the common use of *katha*, *yantra* (in the form of tattoos) and amulets to acquire magical protection in fights with other gangs. Furthermore, she argues that invulnerability (through tattoos, amulets, etc.) is 'perceived as an essential attribute of gang leadership' (2006: 198). Here we have an analysis of the ideas and practices of invulnerability in a hitherto relatively unexplored field of urban youth culture and a telling example of what Turton, in another context, refers to as the 'remarkable resilience of Khon Muang culture' (2006: 170).

At the other end of the 'range of instances' are the older, less aggressive leaders such as irrigation chiefs, headmen, senior monks (*khuba acan*) and millenarian leaders (*phu mi bun*) (Turton 1991a: 163,171). My interpretation of Turton's analysis is that at this end of the spectrum there is much more emphasis on Buddhist morality, merit and meditation as an essential component of invulnerability. Millenarian leaders (*phu mi bun*) in the Northeast, who were attributed powers of invulnerability, stressed the importance of observing moral precepts, and of purification and meditation (ibid. 171). The same can be said of their *ton bun* ('meritorious persons') counterparts of the North. The most famous of these, Khuba Siwichai, was renowned for his building of religious monuments as well as his strict asceticism (including vegetarianism and meditation). The most recent and best known *ton bun* in the North is Khuba Bunchum (considered by some a reincarnation of Khuba Siwichai). He spends long periods during the Buddhist lent (*vassa/phansa*) meditating in remote caves in Burma and even as far as Bhutan. *Ton bun* are attributed a range of supranormal powers, including invulnerability (Cohen 2001). This highlights what has been called the paradox of power in Buddhism: virtuoso, ascetic monks who seek to renounce the world and worldly desires inevitably acquire supranormal powers (*iddhi*) that are world affirming and used by others for mundane ends.

This leads me to Turton's recent biography of a particular Northern monk, Khuba Wajiraphanya (c.1853-1928), who is locally renowned in the Mae Sruay district of Chiang Rai and is still memorialised there through regular *cedi* ceremonies (2006: 160-164). Khuba Wajiraphanya was said to have known and visited Khuba Siwichai, though he himself was not identified locally as a *ton bun*. Nevertheless, he was considered by villagers to be *saksit tae tae* ('most sacred') and to possess a range of supranormal powers. The latter included 'knowledge of "magic" for invulnerability,' imperviousness to being photographed and the capacity to produce or prevent rainfall (ibid. 156). His *kham* knowledge, combined with knowledge of religious texts and secular arts (such as building construction and traditional medicine), made him a prominent local leader (ibid. 157).

Indeed, Turton claims that Khuba Wajiraphanya 'exercised a kind of sovereignty' (ibid. 158) in the region of Mae Sruay. This prompts me to underscore the historical ambivalence of the Thai state towards virtuoso charismatic monks. On the one hand, the state has tended to use such monks as pliant tools to domesticate frontier regions (as in the case of the Acan Man lineage of forest monks in the Northeast); on the other hand, they represent a potential political threat by virtue of their special knowledge and powers and the loyalty of local populations to them. This is evident in the case of Khuba Wajiraphanya who served officially as a Chao Khana Amphur (district ecclesiastic head) in the new Siamese instituted *sangha* administration but at the same time was a dissident advocate of *muang* (Northern Thai) liturgy and contested the authority of the (Siamese) state-appointed local headman (ibid. 158).

Conclusion

Turton has made a significant contribution to our understanding of local leadership in Thailand. His analysis of 'local powers' or 'local power structures' in particular was groundbreaking. Indeed, as he argues, such local realities of power did 'deserve greater theoretical prominence and conceptualisation; they tend to be largely "invisible" in much academic writing, perhaps because they defy analysis in existing paradigms' (1984: 33; 1989a: 88). Turton managed to identify and elucidate these local manifestations of state power by putting ethnographic flesh on the bones of Foucault's concept of the 'micro-physics of power'. He has also made a lasting contribution to the study and our understanding of the limits of state ideological domination in Thailand and of popular culture as a source of dissidence and resistance.

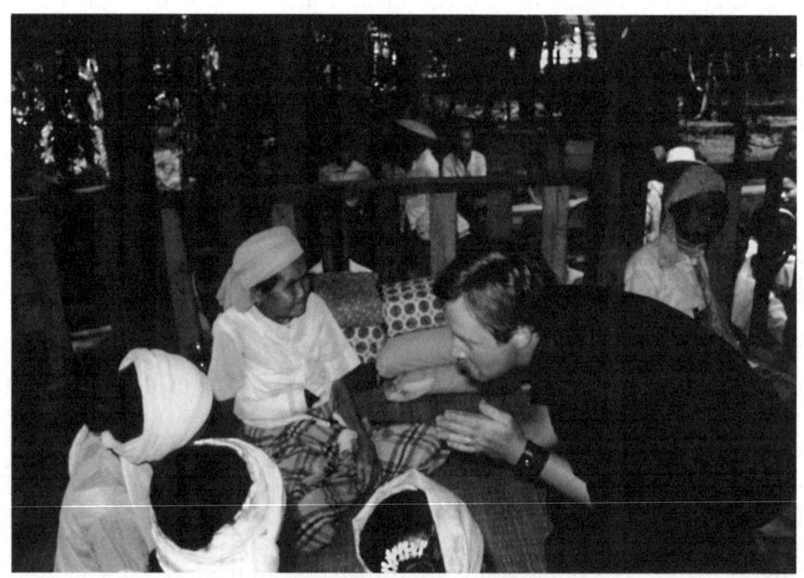

Turton kneeling *wai*-ing a spirit-medium, 1976

4 Roots of Ongoing Conflict: Reflections on Andrew Turton's Analysis of Thailand in the 1970s

Jim Glassman

Introduction

In 1978, responding to the aftermath of the coup of 6 October 1976, a group of Thai scholars produced the volume *Thailand – Roots of Conflict*, published as a special issue of the *Journal of Contemporary Asia* (volume 8, number 1) and also as a book (Turton et al. 1978). Some of the predictions made by the editors of the volume – if they were in fact predictions – seem, with historical retrospect, off base. This is scarcely unusual for work in the social sciences, and indeed what may be one of the deepest illusions held by many social scientists, whatever their political stripe, is that well-done academic work can effectively predict what will happen next (Kolko 2006: 9-12). Certainly if humans have any capacity to make choices, and if social processes are the results of many, many such choices, then prediction seems more like a vain attempt to impose mechanistic intellectual precepts on living agents than a viable scholarly project.

Even with this qualifier, one cannot help but wince when reading statements like the one that concluded the editorial introduction to the *Thailand – Roots of Conflict* volume: 'As the Thai people say, "The longer the sky suppresses, the longer the land resists." The 1980s look set to be a truly revolutionary decade'. One cannot help but wince not only because this statement turned out to be off the mark but, even more so, because in the wake of its failure, a self-satisfied triumphalism on the Right made it difficult to appreciate how many of the issues and problems effectively analysed in these articles remained salient – and how this, in turn, illustrated the ongoing salience of political economic analyses of the Left. In short, the failures of the Thai Left's political project were opportunistically interpreted on the politically victorious Right as proving the irrelevance of the Left's political economy. This intellectual manoeuvre – by helping to exclude the Left's political economy perspectives from most debates in Thailand since the 1980s – has left many analysts of Thailand today bereft of adequate intellectual tools for assessing matters such as the political imbroglio that has engulfed the country since 2005, when military forces descended from those that had launched the 1976 coup and began mobilising to oust the government of Thaksin Shinawatra.

I want to reclaim the articles from the *Roots of Crisis* volume and illustrate some of their continued salience by first placing them in their geographical-historical context and then noting, especially, the important contribution of the piece authored by Andrew Turton, 'The Current Situation in the Thai Countryside' (1978a). I argue that even though much has changed in the countryside since Turton wrote this piece – changes that Turton himself has helped track – there is also much that has remained strikingly similar. Moreover, while social theory necessarily evolves with new struggles, there is also too frequently a strained effort to 'reinvent the wheel' in much analysis of contemporary Thailand, and against this backdrop I suggest that analyses like Turton's might effectively inform our understanding of struggles today, including the political crisis of 2005 to the present.

The *Roots of Conflict* volume in geographical-historical perspective

To appreciate the contribution to Anglophone Thai and Southeast Asian Studies made by the *Roots of Conflict* volume, it is important to emphasize the state of the field as of the 1960s.[1] Before the Vietnam War became a major political issue in the United States, much Southeast Asia scholarship – notwithstanding many remarkable and intellectually valuable works – was marked by a deep political conservatism, some of this informed by Orientalist precepts about Asian Others. Representative in this regard was David Wilson's by now much-maligned claim that Thai peasants were deeply apolitical (1962: 58; cf. Anderson 1978; Bell 1982), a claim very quickly disproved by political events.

A dialectical process connecting protests against the Vietnam War to the aspirations of various dissident scholars began to change this terrain by the late 1960s. Reflective of the changes was the emergence of two new Asian Studies journals committed to promoting radical, left-leaning interpretations of issues in the region – the *Bulletin of Concerned Asian Scholars* (now called *Critical Asian Studies*), founded in 1970, and the *Journal of Contemporary Asia*, also founded in 1970 (Allen 1989; Hewison 2007). The two journals have had, from their inception to the present, overlapping and generally complementary approaches. Based primarily in the United States, the *Bulletin of Concerned Asian Scholars/ Critical Asian Studies* has perhaps placed a slightly greater emphasis on the impact of forces 'external' to Asia, such as US imperialism during the Vietnam War era. Based primarily in the Philippines, the *Journal of Contemporary Asia* has placed a slightly greater emphasis on the impact of forces 'internal' to Asia, such as local and national class processes. While there is always ample scope for differences of opinion as to the relative importance of such forces in any given context, neither journal has been entirely doctrinaire in its approach, and collectively the two began to transform the field of Asian Studies by creating more space for radical and heterodox opinion.

These two journals have, in recent years, been subject to the same commercial pressures as all academic journals: both are now published by Routledge (*Critical Asian Studies* since 2000 under its new name, and the *Journal of Contemporary Asia* since 2006). The varied effects of increased corporate ownership of journals on radical academic work is an important topic that I cannot address here. I note the matter in passing solely because whatever may be the new constraints on attempts by radical academics to find a substantial audience, we should not imagine that these constraints were minimal in the 1960s or 1970s. As a number of reflections on left-leaning analysis of Asia during the Vietnam War era have noted, the environment for production of such work was generally stultifying and even intimidating, with scholars being encouraged by received academic habit to produce work that was either politically irrelevant or conservative (Anderson 1978; Bell 1982). At the same time, the incentive structure and social environment of the academy made it difficult for many younger, radical scholars to produce their work and find their way into rewarding and socially comfortable academic careers (Allen 1989).

Against this backdrop, the production of radical, left-leaning scholarship on Asia was not a trivial accomplishment, and the contributions of the *Roots of Crisis* volume should be placed in this context. Even by the mid-1970s, with the emergence of more radical scholarship throughout the academy, perspectives like those expressed in the *Roots of Crisis* volume were having to prove themselves against considerable institutional inertia, scholarly criticism and even politicised retribution (see e.g. Wikipedia 2008). Moreover, although area studies had begun to transform methodological and theoretical approaches to the study of places like Southeast Asia (Wallerstein et al. 1996: 36-48; Anderson 1998: 9-12), the politics of Asian Studies proved somewhat more challenging to transform than those of fields like Latin American Studies, whose major scholarly organisation was antagonistic to various US imperial ventures in ways that had been far less characteristic of Asian Studies organisations (Chomsky 1988: 204-205; cf. Wakin: 1992).

As a result of the efforts of the new generation of radical Asian scholars in the 1960s and 1970s, the public terrain of intellectual struggle in the Anglophone world was transformed. Bruce Cumings has noted that in the 1950s, when the Korean War broke out, there was little scholarly or journalistic work being done to place the war in a radical or critical interpretive framework – one of the major, honorable exceptions being the courageous and relatively far-sighted work of I.F. Stone

(Cumings 1990: 106-107, 638, 642). By the middle of the 1970s, when the coup in Thailand occurred, people wishing to read critical accounts of such events could find them in a number of places beyond stray newsletters produced by individuals. In 1977, for example, Thadeus Flood published an early and remarkable analysis of the coup in a newsletter for the Indochina Resource Center (1977). In the same year, the *Bulletin of Concerned Asian Scholars* ran an issue with a number of analyses of the coup, including Benedict Anderson's important and much-cited article (1977).

The *Roots of Conflict* issue of the *Journal of Contemporary Asia* built on this body of radical analysis of contemporary events. Most of the articles were not on the coup per se, but attempted to provide the kind of geographical-historical and analytical perspective that could make sense of the coup and ongoing social struggles in Thailand in its wake. The titles of the articles in the volume give a sense of the breadth and depth of the concerns the authors raised as they attempted to anticipate likely future developments by placing the most recent events in the context of longer-term trajectories: 'Thailand and Imperialist Strategy in the 1980s' by Malcolm Caldwell; 'The Socio-Economic Foundation of Modern Thailand' by David Elliott; "Cycles" of Class Struggle in Thailand' by Peter F. Bell; 'Causes and Consequences of the October '76 Coup' by Kraisak Choonhavan (writing under the pen name of Marian Mallet); 'The Current Situation in the Thai Countryside' by Turton; and 'History and Policy of the Communist Party of Thailand' by Patrice de Beer.[2] In what follows, I focus especially on Turton's article, but I also make reference to some of these other pieces, as well as to the general context of their production that I have outlined here.

'The Current Situation in the Thai Countryside' – then

Although Turton's article addressed the situation in the countryside, it in fact did much more than focus on peasants, farmers or rural communities. Turton situated these actors in relation to the broader array of forces at work in Thai society. Indeed, he began with an overview of how Thai agriculture and agrarian social relations had been transformed by the Bowring Treaty of 1855 and tracked many of the changes set in motion by this event up to the 1970s (1978a: 105-6). Turton did devote considerable space to the details of agrarian social life: rural demographics and social structure, rice yields and other such mainstays of agricultural economics occupy an important position in the analysis (ibid. 106 ff.). But Turton also articulated this analysis with a discussion of various aspects of the Thai social structure that must be dealt with in broader political economic terms. For example, Turton noted that generalisations about the incomes of agrarian households and rural regions masked crucial distinctions within these regions – e.g. between local officials and small to medium-scale capitalists on the one side, and households still involved in near-subsistence agriculture, on the other (ibid. 109). Turton was to make much more of these kinds of distinctions in his subsequent work in the 1980s, helping to fill out a detailed and robust picture of the complex social transformations occurring in Thai rural society (e.g. Turton 1989a, b; cf. Hirsch 1989).

While 'The Current Situation in the Thai Countryside' thus focused on many crucial local social relations that articulated agrarian change, it did not neglect broad regional manifestations of these changes – including not only the clearly disadvantaged positions of Northeastern and Northern villagers as a whole (1978a: 108, 112-3) but the ways government policies targeted these regions – both to further ongoing transformations and to suppress opposition (ibid. 115-121). In this context, Turton analysed the activities – and state repression – of the Peasant Federation of Thailand (PFT), one of the most important manifestations during the 1970s of peasants' autonomous capacity to struggle for the improvement of their lives (ibid. 121 ff.). While the PFT was defeated by force, it was an important indicator of both the gnawing inequalities of Thai society and the will of the least privileged to challenge them.

What Turton's analysis of the current situation in the Thai countryside was thus able to do was to map out some of the socio-spatial differentiation occurring as part of counter-insurgency/development, while making a strong case for the ways this geographically-variegated process of class differentiation was contributing to the forms taken by resistance. Turton noted that the PFT developed an especially strong base in the Chiang Mai Valley, where landholding was highly concentrated, and tenancy and indebtedness considerable (1978a: 111-114, 122-125). This crucial observation has been much neglected by subsequent analysts who – following the thinking of the counter-insurgency leaders themselves – have tended to identify discontent solely with groups such as ethnically Lao peasants from the Northeast, 'hill tribes' from the North and Muslim Malays from the South, groups that are portrayed as marginal and as having been 'excluded' from development (cf. Rigg 2003: 162). What Turton's analysis of the PFT clearly showed was that discontent with capitalist development outcomes was being produced precisely among groups that were being fully *included* in development, the very peasants who were being forcibly converted into cash crop farmers, agricultural tenants and farm workers (Glassman 2004a: 65-71).

Like Turton's analysis, other pieces in the *Roots of Conflict* volume brought into focus how development was not merely a technical process that brought new opportunities to the countryside but a deeply political process that stimulated considerable political conflict. Bell's analysis of the 'cycles of struggle', for example, placed the political upheavals of the 1970s in the context of different waves of political struggle throughout the 20th century, thus adding historical depth to the debunking of Wilson's claim about the apolitical character of the Thai peasantry. He also focused specifically on how a number of the rural development schemes promoted as part of counter-insurgency/development were contributing to a further polarization and intensification of conflict (Bell 1978: 62-70). Similarly, Mallet's piece associated the rise of radicalism in the 1970s with not only student activism but also worker and peasant discontent over the conditions of life connected with Thailand's process of development (1978: 80-82).

In all of this process of class-based upheaval, issues of ideological struggle and transformation were clearly of central significance. Although only devoting a few pages to ideological aspects of the conflict, Turton made several observations that have special resonance. Addressing the fact that Thai peasants were typically seen – by Thai elites and American development specialists – as conservative and deferent to the traditional Thai triumvirate of 'nation, religion and king', Turton pointed out that 'villagers have begun to adopt more questioning attitudes, and newer concepts have begun to acquire high or equal priority: democracy, justice, equality, liberty, and national sovereignty' (1978a: 127). Indeed, even within areas such as the Chiang Mai Valley, where considerable repression was exercised by Thai state officials (ibid. 122-123), the emergence of the PFT allowed villagers to become 'more independent, outspoken, and confident' (ibid. 129). In short, Turton was alert to not only the interests of peasants in challenging authority but their ability – in the right circumstances – to do so, and to do so of their own highly conscious accord, a point deserving emphasis in the present moment of political struggles in Northern and Northeastern Thailand.

Indeed, it is in this assertion regarding the interests and consciousness of villagers, I believe, that Turton's analysis of the situation in the 1970s retains its salience. To be sure, much has changed since he wrote this article. Little remains today, for example, that could truly be called subsistence production, and it is probably more accurate to think of most agrarians now as at least semi-commercial farmers rather than simple peasants. Nonetheless, those farmers, like their peasant and PFT forebears, still struggle, using multiple livelihoods (and political) strategies, to limit the incessantly growing gap between their prospects and those of privileged groups in Bangkok as well as among the provincial elite. The triumphalism that overtook much conservative Thai scholarship by the 1980s and 1990s temporarily made this easier to overlook: the 1980s had not become revolutionary and the peasantry had not gone Maoist – indeed most had steered clear of or rejected the Communist Party of Thailand (CPT). Therefore, argued those who were satisfied, the regional and social disparities that had agitated some analysts so much were not as crucial as they were made out to be – indeed, they were inevitable and temporary – and Thailand could now concentrate on becoming the next 'tiger' or 'newly industrialising country' (see e.g. Muscat 1994: 248).

But the 1990s were to prove nearly as cruel to the celebrants of capitalist victory as the 1980s had proved to those who hoped for capitalist defeat. Amid both booming growth and booming disparities, new rounds of social struggles emerged with renewed vigour – those of Bangkok workers (Glassman 2004a: 101-104), Northeast farmers (Somchai 2006) and villagers throughout the country whose livelihoods were being destroyed by development projects (Missingham 2004). Then the boom went bust, leaving many struggling not only to recover but to explain. And while the bust also forced forms of restructuring that helped weaken many of the renewed social struggles, it also made clear that Thailand's development trajectory was never going to be smooth and conflict-free (Bell 2003; Glassman 2004a: 174-202).

'The Current Situation in the Thai Countryside' – now

Indeed, many of the kinds of savage disparities Turton had outlined, and the social struggles they helped produce, have become yet more salient amid the recent changes in Thailand. Indicative here is the way Thaksin Shinawatra's Thai Rak Thai (TRT) Party was able to build broad support for an agenda that promised to redress many of these inequalities. While TRT started out as a party of big business, it made itself a formidable force by enrolling both many of the small and medium-scale rural businesses whose importance Turton had noted earlier and – sometimes through such actors – the much broader communities of farmers and villagers whose fortunes had not been well served by either the boom or the bust (Glassman 2004b; Pasuk & Baker 2004: 80-82; Ungpakorn 2007: 16-17). Certainly, not all had remained the same in the countryside since the 1970s. Overall, in spite of highly uneven development, material standards of living had generally improved, in part because counter-insurgency/development had in fact bequeathed some material benefits, in part because there was eventually some 'trickle down' from urban-industrial growth, and in part because numerous villagers migrated in increased numbers to Bangkok and elsewhere for industrial employment, while their households learned to get by through increasingly diversified economic strategies (Glassman 2004a: 160-161). None of this, however, prevented an ongoing process of polarization that left increasing numbers of people up-country feeling even poorer relative to better-off groups that included most Bangkok middle classes (ibid. 161-168).

At the same time, and in part because of the efforts of rural and urban working class groups (Ungpakorn 1997; Ockey 2004), new democratic spaces were opened in Thailand by the end of the period of economic boom (from 1986 to 1996). Within these spaces, those who had benefited less from the boom began to register a number of demands, ranging from higher wages and better working conditions to maintenance of rural livelihoods and control over the resources necessary for this (Hirsch 2001; Glassman 2002, 2004a: 102-103; Missingham 2004). In addition, with the opening of more parliamentary space, the kinds of rural political leaders who had been spawned by the processes Turton described began to descend on Bangkok, using the state and their majority constituencies as a means by which to try to extract more resources for themselves and their backers (McVey 2000). Conservative and traditional elites within the national state contrived a number of means to try to limit the new forms of political participation by subaltern groups, while Bangkok middle classes grumbled about the rather sordid image of a Thai democracy putatively subverted by rural political bosses (Pasuk & Sungsidh 1994). By 1997, these tensions were ingrained within the new constitution, a document that managed to protect many forms of traditional authority, including that of the monarchy, while institutionalising in limited forms some of the gains made by social movement actors earlier in the decade (Connors 2007, 2008).

Against this backdrop, Thaksin and TRT ended up posing a challenge to specific forms of elite power. Using the backing he could get from villagers for TRT's 'populist' programmes in the countryside, Thaksin gained a considerable hold on portions of the state. Notably, his approach was entrepreneurial and openly pro-capitalist, promising villagers support for their commercial activities and opportunities to become rich like the prime minister himself (Pasuk & Baker 2004: 112-118). This was not an approach that played well with rural groups that remained committed to direct class struggle, such as members of the Northern Farmers Network, fighting to gain title to the land of absentee landlords in Lamphun in the Chiang Mai Valley (Glassman 2004b: 52). But for a number of other agrarian groups, TRT policies at least offered forms of economic support – such as debt moratoriums and loans, not to mention the highly popular national health insurance scheme – that had not been on offer before. As such, TRT consolidated considerable popularity within rural areas of the North and Northeast (Somchai 2008; Walker 2008).

Yet popularity was not enough to preserve Thaksin's regime. To deliver the goods to the countryside, TRT had to begin co-opting or displacing some of the local state leaders who had come to power within the Cold War state. This put TRT on a collision course with royalists in the Thai state, especially when Thaksin began to try to replace the military-administrative structures of the South (McCargo 2005, 2006). While Thaksin's regime had committed numerous human rights abuses and violations of civil liberties that would have provided ample basis for legitimate popular opposition (Glassman 2004b; Pasuk & Baker 2004: 144-167), most of Thai society remained mute on these issues until royalist and elite sentiment turned against Thaksin in 2005 (Kasian 2006; Thongchai 2008; Ukrist 2008). Indeed, even some of Thaksin's most egregious policies, such as the extrajudicial slaughter of more than two thousand people during the 2003 'war on drugs,' may have gained him a certain popularity among those who saw him as a decisive leader attempting to deal with social problems (Walker 2008: 100). More generally, whatever people in the countryside liked or disliked about Thaksin, they saw the TRT government as providing some forms of support that addressed their concerns about long-standing Bangkok-centrism, as well as about corrupt and violent local leaders, who they hoped would lose power in the context of the TRT state's attempt to create new patronage networks (Somchai 2008; Walker 2008).

This was not the view of either the royalists or the Bangkok middle classes, and they thus played a central role in backing the military ouster of Thaksin's government in 2006 (Pasuk & Baker 2008; Ukrist 2008) as well as in destabilising the People's Power Party (PPP) government, which was elected in late 2007 on the strength of its association with TRT policies (Glassman 2009). In short, as Thailand's development processes have evolved, the growing, class-based divide within the country, with its profound and obvious spatial dimensions, has completely overtaken intellectually lazy, modernisation-theoretic and neoliberal assumptions about the natural flowering of democracy in a context of 'free markets'. In this sense, the socio-spatial polarization of Thailand that Turton highlighted in 1978 has evolved even further, and the failure of mainstream social theorists to adequately comprehend its basis and significance when they dismissed arguments like those put forward in the *Roots of Crisis* volume has come back to haunt them.

Conclusion

In 2008, the *Journal of Contemporary Asia* devoted a special issue to the 2006 coup in Thailand, the first full issue of the journal devoted to Thailand since its *Roots of Crisis* collection twenty years earlier. As the editors of the 2008 special issue, Michael K. Connors and Kevin Hewison, noted (2008, 2):

> The articles of the 1978 special issue focused on ... the unprecedented social divisions and class struggles that had been revealed

> ... That a second *Journal of Contemporary Asia* special issue on
> Thailand should be produced following another coup is entirely
> appropriate. Thaksin Shinawatra, the only Thai prime minister
> to win two successive general elections, was overthrown on 19
> September 2006. Projecting himself as the political saviour of
> the domestic capitalist class following the 1997 economic melt-
> down, Thaksin led a political party that had changed the nature
> of Thailand's politics while also generating remarkable divisions
> within the country.

Yet Thaksin's regime did not merely create remarkable divisions; it both
remade and exacerbated older ones, including Thailand's intertwined
class and urban-rural divides.

In this sense, even though the PFT and CPT have long since collapsed
and been displaced by right-wing populist political structures, the struggles that animated their existence have continued into the present
(Hewison & Rodan 1994). And what is illustrated by Thailand's current
political imbroglio is that if these struggles do not gain expression
through leftist parties and organisations committed to progressive political transformations, like the PFT, then they will gain expression through
actions such as attempts of opportunist populists to capture and use
those struggles. Indeed, the increasingly loud expression of discontent in
the North and Northeast since 2006 at the policies and preferences of
the coup makers in Bangkok speaks to the continuing relevance of the re-
gionalised social divisions Turton analysed in the 1970s (see Keyes, this
volume). Moreover, while numerous foreign observers continue to be
dazzled by images of love for the King, a not-so-subtle subtext of distaste
for the ways royalism is used to subvert democracy has become readily
evident to those who care to look (Glassman, forthcoming). The mere
fact that TRT/PPP have repeatedly won elections, even when they are understood to be disliked by the royalists, and that charges of lèse majesté
are once again being liberally used against any and all perceived opponents of royalist power, indicates that values such as democracy and social justice are coming into conflict with the privileges maintained by
elites through traditional forms of institutional authority. As Turton and
his co-authors in the *Roots of Crisis* volume rightly noted, Thai villagers
are not incapable of developing quite critical perspectives on power, and
indeed it is in their interests to do so.

Turton's analysis of the severe socio-spatial class divide in Thailand,
and the political-ideological possibilities this generates, is thus an important and enduring contribution, as I see it. Turton's conclusions,
while far more conditional than those of the lead editorial in the *Roots
of Conflict* volume, also pointed to the prospects for revolutionary struggle: 'If the opposition, and crucially the poor peasants and their allies,

make this [revolutionary] choice then it is hard to see how the conflict could be resolved without armed struggle of a qualitatively new kind and level of intensity' (1978a: 135). Of course, with historical hindsight, we can say that although the armed struggle did briefly intensify in the late 1970s, not as many peasants made this choice as the CPT might have hoped, and some relatively adroit 'velvet-glove' counter-insurgency strategies implemented from 1978 onwards by the Thai state in fact prevented the revolutionary struggle from reaching the level of intensity that the CPT had hoped it would reach (Gawin 1990). But the fact that the revolution did not occur has not relieved Thailand from having to deal with social problems like those Turton so carefully outlined.

A comforting myth beloved of capitalist planners is that the problems of capitalism – uneven development, growing social disparity, political conflict and so on – are fundamentally external to the system, caused by loathed 'Others' who range from 'terrorists' and communist infiltrators to criminals and 'welfare cheats'. This comforting mythology is just that; many of capitalist societies' most crucial social problems are entirely 'endogenous', generated out of the social struggles that are central to capitalist development. Even if the loathed 'Others' disappear or their institutions collapse – as with the PFT and the CPT – the problems and social struggles generated by capitalist social relations will remain, in Thailand as elsewhere in the world.

Turton's analysis of Thai society in the 1970s powerfully highlighted these problems internal to capitalism: the growth of the PFT and the CPT was not their cause but their expression. When the PFT and CPT collapsed, the form of expression of those struggles changed, mutating further as the rural social structures in which many of them were embedded were further transformed by capitalist development. Like Turton himself, social scientists studying current Thai social conflicts will have to continually build and adapt their analytical tools, but they have no reason to abandon the crucial insights about the enduring features of social struggles that Turton called attention to three decades ago.

Notes

1   I focus here, for reasons of the limits of my own competence and familiarity, solely on the English-language scholarship on Thailand and Southeast Asia. This includes work by scholars not only from the Anglophone world but scholars from elsewhere writing in English. Needless to say, this cannot be taken to adequately represent what was being written in other languages.

2   The identity of Marian Mallett was only revealed as Kraisak Choonhavan, a well-known scholar and political figure in Thailand, in 2008 at the ICTS Conference where the chapters in this book were first presented, by Andrew Turton with Kraisak's permission. [Eds.]

Turton dancing with Thai woman in Lumpini, 1 May 1976

5 Censorship and Authoritative Forms of Discourse: A Reconsideration of Thai Constructions of Knowledge

Nicholas Tapp

Introduction: coherence

In this paper I attempt to locate Andrew Turton's work (notably Turton 1984; 1991b) within the context of a post-structuralist mode of social inquiry which was replacing earlier assumptions of social and cultural homogeneity. The trend away from a purely class-oriented analysis in Turton's work at this time was typical if not prophetic of new understandings of Thailand as a rapidly changing, dynamic and complex society, and his emphasis on the power of dominant forms of discourse as well as the exceptions to this in popular consciousness and practice has continued to prove salient to appreciations of the role of information control and censorship in the Thaksin era. These works can be understood not only in terms of the changing nature of Thai society but also in terms of a general theoretical shift towards interpretive approaches in anthropology. Some recent approaches, which I examine in conclusion, seem bound to an interpretive mode of analysis while having lost some of the rootedness this earlier work had in an analysis of the suppressed and subordinated, with its faith in the importance of the unrecognised. At the same time, new moves toward a post-hegemonic understanding of power – of power understood as a kind of potentiality – ironically reflect the same kind of discomfort with totalisation that Turton's works considered here displayed.

Turton's work has probably always been deeply concerned with the interface of the elite with the popular, or local, and in the introduction to the co-edited collection *Thai Constructions of Knowledge* (Manas & Turton 1991), this was expressed particularly clearly, in a new mode that became paradigmatic for studies of Thai society that followed it. Here we find the concern expressed with 'what becomes interesting, useful and proper to know', and a focus outlined on 'how topics and discourses become authorised, constructed, regulated, suppressed, and subverted'. These theoretical orientations were outlined against a backdrop of current analyses of Thai society itself and its changing historical formations. The argument was against 'the idea of a unitary, essential Thai culture' based on 'fundamental cultural axioms or principles'. The work raised the question of what, given the Foucauldian connections of power with knowledge taken up in this work, makes particular forms of knowledge, textualised or otherwise, 'doxic', in Bourdieu's sense of that which makes the natural and social worlds appear self-evident to us (1977: 167), which 'goes without saying because it comes without saying'. It also raised the question of whether it is the case that those forms of knowledge that tend towards the 'unstatable' are thereby, since they are less explicit, less contestable? So the attention is turned to the power of rhetoric, where the work of Maurice Bloch (1975) on formal rhetorical political speech in its Bernsteinian 'restrictive code' aspects is referred to, and discourse is located within a continuum, from poetics towards political speech, and then towards political executions and extrajudicial killings, seen as examples of the force resorted to when the persuasion required for hegemonic domination fails.

Turton's own article in this collection is crucial, for here he outlined his discomfort, although it is a respectful one, with Tambiah's unitary structuralist model of ideological coherence of disparate elements in village spirit worship (1970); there may in fact be real cognitive dissonance, Turton argues, when villagers take off their amulets before performing Buddhist rites (1991a). Catherine Bell (1989, 1992) ably sketched a new phase of religious studies in her description of the postmodern paradigms of heterogeneity and dissonance that replaced earlier structuralist coherences. And in Turton's article in this collection (1991a) one could see this new phase clearly signalled, with constant reference to the ideas of invulnerability which, Turton suggests, may form some kind of response to power, and to the 'immobilising' effects of fear and silence that mechanisms of social exclusion and terror, associated with powerful forms of domination, bring about. Notions of invulnerability, as he had said previously, are crucial if fear can be seen as mediating 'between coercion and consent' in a society (1984), and such an approach was predicated on the vision of a complex society in which dominant ideas could be contested. In *Thai Constructions of Knowledge* (*TCK*), Thai society itself is painted in terms of fragmentations and dissonances, contradictions and heterogeneities ('heterogeneity, decentredeness, dispersal, fragmentation'), in startling contrast to earlier paradigms of Thai society in terms of changeless consistency and cultural homogeneity. It was this of course which led to Turton's later work on ethnicity and social identities in Thailand (2000).

However, many of these concerns had been flagged much earlier, in the short introduction to the (1984) collection *History and Peasant Consciousness in Southeast Asia*, which was written together with Shigeharu Tanabe (Turton & Tanabe 1984b), and in Turton's own major article in that collection ('Limits of Ideological Domination and the Formation of Social Consciousness'). Many of the remarks in this article are so topical that it is needful to remind oneself that it was written some time before 1984. Here we have the direct attempt to engage critically with theories of ideology in the context of the Thai social formation, a social formation which, it was becoming increasingly clear, could not be reduced in any simplistic way to the mechanisms of exclusively defined classes as they had been classically understood (Laclau 1977; Laclau & Mouffe 1985, 2001).[1] It is here that the project to look at the 'relation between ideological and other forms of domination or subjectification or reification' was announced, and this was explicitly associated with how we were to understand the changing nature of Thai society, and the question of the 'relative autonomy of local communities' in their relationship with the state, both in fact and as a 'cognitive/ideological construction' (Turton & Tanabe 1984b). There is great attention paid here to the apparently successful way in which, in Thailand, alternative forms of discourse appeared to have been 'co-opted' by the state, and to the dialectical relations between forms of dominance, persuasion and consent. A Gramscian model of hegemony was adopted, which forced the attention not just towards local institutions, but also towards 'non-institutional, informal, extra-judicial ... social forces' (Turton 1984). Here already we were enjoined not only to focus on fixed or structured forms of identity, but on 'fragmented, less articulate, and everyday forms of popular culture and consciousness' (Turton & Tanabe 1984b). There is a constant concern with creativity – with what has since then come to be called 'agency' – in many of these statements, and at the same time with informal power structures at the local level, typified by such apical figures as thugs, spies and informers.[2] What really could be more salient or important in the Thaksin era, when we saw an effective silencing of media debate under the guise of a self-censored 'free press' (see Thitinan 1997; Ubonrat 2007), itself challenged by the reversion to an earlier and more overt form of militaristic state force?

Consciousness

Although difficult to summarise in its reach, the 'Limits of Ideological Domination' article particularly highlighted the 'constitution' (and 'reconstitution'!) of social subjects through ritual discourse, such as 'rituals of expulsion' and inclusion, from *suukhwan* ('calling the spirits') to 'Village Scout' rituals, the importance of understanding 'local power structures', and the prevalence of violence in Thai society.

Nobody perhaps has yet really come to grips with a genuine analysis of these local forms of power so prevalent in Thailand and some neighbouring countries, associated with magical beliefs and masculinity and status, tattooing and blessing and, indeed, beliefs in 'invulnerability'.[3]

Yet these discussions of state ideology and popular forms of resistance and autonomy certainly pointed research towards this direction. Here we had something of a framework for the theoretical understanding and analysis of mechanisms of violence and consent within a historical framework. The struggle of Turton and others in this field has perhaps constantly been against both a kind of 'culturalism', which was seen to be the result of a certain kind of conservative anthropology concerned with the reproduction of social forms, and at the same time against a dominating nationalist rhetoric in Thailand, which constantly sought to downplay the realities of social difference in the interests of a common assumed unity. It has now become almost commonplace to see culture as a site of struggle, and the older disciplinary boundaries between politics and culture, economics and ritual have largely broken down or dissolved entirely in new understandings of the politics of cultural difference.[4] Yet in the Thai, and wider, context, I would argue that the work of Turton has been fundamental in opening paths and guiding the way towards new forms of engaged research, more nuanced understandings of historical processes, and the mechanisms of social exclusion and inclusion, accommodation and resistance that build up a complex and highly differentiated society.

What has interested me particularly as a result of all this, and in my own work, has been the attempt to understand tacit or implicit forms of knowledge, which have exercised indeed many anthropologists and social scientists. It seems clear that the old 'dominant ideology' thesis, associated with a functionalist Marxism, had much in common with classic anthropological understandings of society and culture which tended to depict them as seamless wholes, unitary bodies with – as Turton says in the introduction to *TCK* – fundamental guiding principles of an explicit and articulate kind. The primacy of assumptions of 'false consciousness' that arose from the holistic thesis of a monolithic, dominant ideology was modified on the one hand by Gramsci, who pointed to the importance of what he called 'common sense' as a fragmentary discourse of scattered folk perceptions that could not always be made into the sort of seamless wholes beloved of elites, and on the other by Althusser, who showed ideology as working not only through the repressive apparatus of the state, but also through other everyday 'ideological state apparatuses' such as the family, media, church or school, and moreover working at a semi-conscious and barely realised level, to constitute its 'subjects'.[5] To that duo, who broadened and expanded the notion of ideology beyond formal state structures and beyond the level of conscious awareness, we should add Foucault. Foucault has been a major influence on Turton and colleagues in many ways, but let us just consider him here as yet another theorist who showed us the 'unconscious' workings of ideological 'discourse' in its materiality and practical implications, in our everyday lives. And Raymond Williams' notion of the 'structure of feeling', that 'particular sense of life' or 'community of experience hardly needing expression' (1961) was another important influence on the approach to ideology and consciousness considered here, marking a new reconsideration of the role of emergent cultural activities in potentially transforming or changing formal social structures.[6]

Space and architecture are of course primary arenas in which this kind of semi-conscious, ideologically informed knowledge has been shown to particularly express itself, and Turton's earlier work on domestic architecture in North Thailand showed an awareness of this (1978b). Bourdieu's work on the Kabyle house was similarly influential in constructing a theory of the *habitus* that was largely unconscious, or 'doxic' as Turton was later to put it (Bourdieu 1977, 1979; Turton 1991b). Gramsci's notion of 'common sense' was as something fragmentary and incoherent, full of contradictions and incoherencies which to some extent escaped the frameworking of dominant ideologies, since it was partly based on a direct perception of the world and tied to practical activity in the world. This opened a space for the reconsideration of popular knowledge as potentially liberating, a contrast Bloch (1977, 1991) was also to build on his argument for a radical difference between a socially determined 'ritual consciousness' and unideological 'practical' knowledge, although to some extent this still reflected the older positivistic Marxian divisions between 'science' and 'ideology'.[7] For Gramsci, 'common sense' might be found in folk tales and folk perceptions, myths and fragmented memories, songs, superstitions and proverbs of varying truth value, and while expressing a habituated view of society and the world, was potentially free from susceptibility to the bricolaging activities of dominant ideologies, as a result precisely of the 'unsystematicness' which – as Turton remarked in the *TCK* article on 'Invulnerability and local knowledge' (1991a) – may be the 'normal condition of popular knowledge'. It was in that unsystematicness of popular wisdom, then, that some ability to contest the dominant representations of power might perhaps be located. Just how 'doxic' was this practical, or popular, consciousness, and to what extent did it form an implicit critique of dominant social forms?

On the one hand, then, we had an argument tending towards a new view of practical common sense and popular consciousness as potentially escaping the bounds of the ideological, something in touch with what Margaret Archer (2000) calls the orders of nature and practice, after a more Gramscian than a Foucauldian model. On the other hand, we had Clifford Geertz – the American cultural anthropologist and harbinger of the new turn towards an 'interpretive' anthropology which some have glossed as post-modern – arguing for common sense as deeply ideological, in the older sense of that term, as precisely that which is, as Turton said it might be, uncontestable because it is so deep-rooted in our psyches and everyday practices (Geertz 1983a). Geertz's view had more in common with Foucault than with Gramsci and, as with much of Foucault's work, raised the question of how social change could ever occur, what were the limits indeed of an ideologically conditioned and coloured view of the world. If state-sanctioned force and violence could be seen as marking the breakdown of hegemonic power, might popular consciousness be approached as a kind of repository of passive resistance to the domination of the powerful, or did it mark an even deeper encroachment of the ideological into the very fabric of our everyday lives?

One of the best examples I know of the kind of unsystematic, deep-rooted tacit or habitual knowledge of which Geertz and in a different way Foucault both spoke, comes from Chinese ethnography, in an article by Xin Liu on the cave dwellings of Shaanxi (1998), which showed how implicit social hierarchies (between seniors and juniors, men and women), which were reflected in the habitual use of domestic space (like seating arrangements), remained almost entirely untouched by the efforts of the Maoist revolution to radically disrupt and alter such hiererachies, precisely because they were so silent, accepted, unthought and unspoken. That kind of silence of course is quite different from the silence that results from fear and intimidation, of which Turton (1984) speaks often, the '*khit ork phuut mai ork*' of the weak farmer confronted by the powerful official.[8] Yet it reaches to a further depth of tacit, implicit, popular knowledge and ways of being that Turton's work also often touches. Indeed Xin Liu expresses his awareness of the strength of such unarticulated consciousness, if we can call it consciousness at all, when he begins his article with a quotation from Bourdieu: 'It is because agents never know completely what they are doing that what they do has more sense than they know' (Bourdieu 1990).

And of course that perception is itself deeply sociological, speaking of a profound depth of unawareness which calls for analysis rather than description, and for explanation rather than mere understanding. As Stephan Feuchtwang (1975) once put it, 'If social relations were self-evident there would be no need for social science'. Some form of 'false consciousness' assumptions are indeed embedded in mainstream social theory itself, without any necessary recourse to Marxist paradigms.[9] Although we have been talking here more about a level of knowledge that is partially conscious, partially unconscious, something like an iceberg partially submerged, this also involves the assumption of a level at which actors may not realise why or how they really behave. It is awareness of these levels of suppressed, unreflected, or simply unrealised consciousness which, I think, much so-called 'postmodern' analysis misses, and I return to this point in the final section of this paper.

The attempt to archaeologically excavate such depths of perception, or semi-perception, raised important questions about the 'textuality' or otherwise of discourse, and pointed towards the importance of oral narration techniques and folk transmissions of knowledge in a way which has maybe paralleled the swing in social theory towards first an anthropology of practice, and then an anthropology of embodiment. Again Turton signalled this swing very clearly when he spoke of techniques of 'manual knowledge', in reference to Viggo Brun's work (Turton 1984).[10] Later this kind of embodied consciousness was to be referred back to the notion of 'social memory' which became popular in the works of Connerton (1989) and Fentress and Wickham (1992), and somewhat similarly could be seen as a site of passive resistance to dominant powerful interests. Xin Liu's example is interesting, though, because while the unreflective continuation of everyday spatial practices might be seen as a 'doxic' resistance to social change, to the extent that revolutionary change was here imposed from the outside and with massive state sanction, it might also be seen as a form of passive resistance or 'weapon of the weak', in Scott's sense (1985).

With somewhat similar concerns, Bloch (1982, 1986) was to make good use of Dan Sperber's (1985) work on semi-propositional 'representational' beliefs, like convictions or culturally bound assumptions, which might be only half-understood and therefore not of a verifiable, 'propositional' type. Bloch put forward an argument that ritual could not properly be understood either by intellectualist approaches which treated ritual as a statement, as 'saying something' about the world, or by functionalist approaches which saw ritual as an action, as a kind of activity, 'doing something' in the world. In actuality, ritual was neither statement nor action, but something in between. Back in 1975, Sperber had talked of the importance of 'tacit knowledge', which he saw as either 'implicit' in the sense that it can be made explicit, or 'unconscious', in understanding cultural symbolism. He also distinguished an 'encyclopediac' knowledge (of the world) from the 'semantic' knowledge (of categories), and argued that 'symbolic knowledge' was something in between, a kind of learning and remembering, both ritual and verbal, and not wholly expressible semantically (1975: 108). These distinctions between habitual or embodied knowledge and our more cognitive theoretical knowledge continue to be salient in cognitive anthropology and neural psychology (Bloch 1991), and the related distinctions between 'insider' and 'outsider' knowledges of a society, tacit and more 'experience-distant' forms of knowledge (Geertz 1983b) not necessarily related to membership of a society, continue to be discussed.

Returning to Bourdieu's remark about what agents do having more sense than they know, which reiterates a classic sociological view as well as general theories of false consciousness, it may also be taken to be a presumptuous one – that somehow we as analysts, as social experts, must know better than the people who talk to us why it is that they do the things they do; there is a privileged insight that belongs to the analyst rather than to the social actor who must remain mystified and confused. And that, of course, raises the whole question of the authority to speak for the subaltern, which has been most intensively discussed in the context of South Asian studies, a field Turton has been very aware of. Passing over Spivak's notorious remarks about this in the various versions of her speech questioning the possibility of resurrecting a genuinely subaltern voice at all (e.g. 1988), more recently Hansen (1997) has provided a useful overview of the subaltern debate and how the programme to generate an indigenous voice was itself heir to what he calls a 'romanticist communitarian discourse born in the West'. Hansen is positing a Hegelian kind of dialectic which took place through colonialism, in which images of homogeneous autarkic local communities were constantly being constructed by contrast with representations of the dominant West as Other, as modern and progressive and advanced – images of autarky, which then became necessary sites of struggle and articulation in resistance to those impositions of state-related forms of power and authority, in what Spivak (1988b) called a 'strategic essentialism'; and then these images of unequal power relations were being refracted onto the image of the social scientist with his (yes, 'his') informants and interlocutors (Hansen 1997). I think an awareness of subaltern studies has been important in Turton's own work, as too the familiarity with South American projects stemming from liberation theology and the work of cultural theorists like the late Leo Alting von Gesau, to give voice to the marginal and repressed, and to articulate the unarticulated and perhaps inexpressible. Here social science found another role: to reveal the hidden structures of exploitation and oppression by articulating forms of cultural consciousness in which a critique of those structures had been hidden, but at the same time needed to remain acutely self-conscious of the dangers of commandeering what should ideally be an indigenous project of liberation from conditioned thinking.

All of this leads us to a situation in which it becomes more important than ever to discuss openly the freedom or monopoly of the press in Thailand, to reactivate suppressed memories of the 1976 coup as Thongchai (2002) did, to debate the role of the monarchy and its continued relevance and the strangely arbitrary laws of lèse majesté. The processes of co-optation and censorship, of appropriation and domination, of violence and consent, to which Turton's work has constantly drawn attention, have perhaps never been so salient as today, in the very fierce struggle that continues to take place between what one may still fairly unblushingly call reactionary and progressive forces. These struggles are now very largely about what 'may' be said and what 'may not' be said. It is perhaps when compromise and accommodation become impossible that power is handed, not to the people, but to extrajudicial factions among the people that support certain tendencies within Thai society rather than others (Anderson 1977, 1990; cf. Anderson 1978), as we saw in the *krathing daeng* or 'Red Gaurs' of the 1970s, in the very terrible killings and accusations that characterised the 2003/4 'war on drugs', and in the complete breakdown of communicative public space which has resulted in the use of force in the South.[11] Indeed it might be argued that it was precisely Thaksin's resort to popular might[12] that opened the way for his own removal by military force. In terms of theories of social violence, Turton's work has been fundamental in alerting us to the importance of these normally suppressed issues of violence and coercion in the Thai context, and their intimate relations with tacit understandings and silences, strategic or otherwise. What is particularly at issue here is those covert processes of subterfuge and silent refusals to participate, these alternative spaces of identity formation and construction of unorthodox perspectives, which much analysis misses.

Interpretive approaches

Some recent views appear to eschew analysis of this nature in favour of a kind of appeal to populism. An article by Yoshinori Nishizaki (2007) compares rural views of corrupt politicians in Thailand to the way Marcos or the Burmese junta leaders may be perceived as 'rural heroes' by farmers in villages.[13] Despite the corruption scandals known to surround the well-known figure of politician (and former prime minister) Banharn Silpa-Archa, Yoshinori stresses that he is seen as a benevolent *pho muang* by some.[14] In a view that is admittedly social constructionist and is akin to a stance of ethnomethodological 'indifference' (Garfinkel 1967), the argument is that there is no 'essentially' depraved or benevolent Banharn; it is all spin (that is my gloss) – what matters is how moral authority is constructed at the village and provincial levels, through the kind of village ceremonies and meetings with school children the article well describes.[15] This is largely a matter of visibility. Villagers are 'agnostic' about Banharn's corruption, Yoshinori argues, because they do not *see* it, but they treat him as a 'virtuous leader' because this is what they *do* see. Yoshinori explicitly criticises 'false consciousness' arguments and the condescension of arguments that villagers need educating in what democracy really means, and he specifically disagrees with Turton's 'limits of ideological domination' argument (1984) and with Scott's account (1985) of covert forms of resistance. This seems to imply that Yoshinori (in a perhaps Foucauldian way) believes there *are*

no limits to ideological domination, that 'ideology' is in effect all we
have, and hence constitutes a complete rejection of the sort of debates
we find in, for example, Butler, Laclau and Žižek (2000). Butler refers
there, for instance, to the '*incompleteness* of subject-formation hegemony
requires' (Butler et al. 2000: 5; my italics). And that admission of incompleteness in theories of hegemony is vitally important, because it
does open a space for creative reinterpretation and renewals beyond the
limits of what is normally accepted as natural and inevitable. It seems
to me the kind of approach represented by this description of rural understandings of authority begs important questions of truth and levels
of analysis that are barely touched on by such descriptive accounts.[16]

An article by Andrew Walker (2008) puts this in a much broader perspective. This is similarly a critique of the 'negative portrayal of rural
electoral culture' and the view (by both political commentators and the
recent coup leaders) that support for Thaksin provided 'clear evidence
of voter irrationality'. It is a critique of the view that the 'Thai populace
lacks the basic characteristics essential for a modern democratic society'
– a view that Walker, in other articles (2001, 2004) as well, also associ-
ates partly with the communitarian valorisation of rural culture as
against its commercialisation and the injection of large amounts of (as
he sees it, necessary) cash into the rural economy, and it forms a rous-
ing dismissal of the view of 'gormless' rural voters and a 'failed democratic electorate'. Here the argument, following Kerkvliet (2002, 2005),
is for a broader understanding of local politics as involving debate and
cooperation between groups and individuals over local resource alloca-
tion and the values that underpin it and, following Nidhi (2003) on the
role of an unwritten 'cultural constitution' in Thailand, that these local
values embody a sort of 'rural constitution', which is what shapes the
processes of local elections and political behaviour.[17] Relations with the
state are mediated through culturally embedded actors, argues Walker
(2008). The very skilful ethnography in this piece shows us how local
voters do indeed appear to particularly value leaders who are local, and
will therefore understand local priorities, and how they expect various
forms of assistance besides monetary assistance from their representatives. They expect a certain amount of personal aggrandisement by their
leaders, but not too much; and in the case of Thaksin they took considerable pride in the economic achievements of the country and in his
good English, which was seen as a sign of the educational status also
much valued in the local perspective. Thaksin was also admired, says
Walker, for his campaigns such as the 'war on drugs', which received
considerable local support and commendation.

It seems to me that the approach here (as in Yoshinori's article) owes
something to Turton's longstanding arguments for precisely this sort of
attention to the detail of local situations, yet the conclusions seem to re-

flect local ideological misapprehensions in a somewhat mimetic way, with no attempt (in true postmodern style) to ask where truth may actually lie, or perhaps more pertinently, to probe alternatives to the dominant perspective, alternatives that may be barely discernible and certainly not overt.[18] Besides local institutions of the state, the call in Turton and Tanabe (1984b) was to look particularly at 'non-institutional, informal, extra-judicial, sometimes illegal and subterranean, social forces, processes, and milieux'. But there is no attempt in these more recent works to deal, for example, with the power of fear and intimidation, to come to terms with the surveillance capacities of the modern state, or its powers to terrorize and the capacities of violence that the 'war on drugs' unleashed at the local level throughout rural Thailand. That was an instructive case, for it was not just a matter of concerned village elders and a feckless minority of youth, criminals, ethnic minorities or other scapegoats, but a matter of very real conflicts and disputes, hatreds and enmities between different individuals and indeed different categories of individuals at the local level who resorted happily to the violence that had suddenly been legitimated, and therefore unleashed, in order to settle longstanding scores that ran beneath the surface of village life. The appalling excesses of this time have been well documented, with cases of the planting of drugs on victims after their deaths, the killing of children, and local police fulfilling their quotas. In many areas there was open licence to shoot and kill those who stood in the way of particular alliances between local officials, police and drug dealers. In Khek Noi, a large Hmong settlement in Phitsanalouk which I revisited towards the end of 2003, extrajudicial killings had become almost the norm and an atmosphere of utter terror reigned.

In such recent literature there seems to be a worrying unconcern with what Williams (1977, 1980 in Turton 1984) called 'selective traditions' and with what Therborn (1980 in Turton 1984) described as *exclusions* from discourse, 'restrictive' practices such as scapegoating and 'excommunication', the complexities of actual consciousness at any one time as a 'multiply determined configuration of elements'. There is a refusal to confront or even recognise the relations between domination, persuasion and consent and the more structural aspects of power, indeed to deal with what Craig Reynolds (in his article in *Thai Constructions of Knowledge*; Reynolds 1991) importantly called, in a literary context, 'state poetics' (the rules about what can be said) which have become too diffuse to be grasped at all. Perhaps what is missing is class analysis. Perhaps that has just become too difficult, and too complex, for a largely interpretive anthropology.

Conclusions: power

Scott Lash (2007) has recently written interestingly on a post-hegemonic phase of social understanding, in reference to Negri's interpretation (1991) of Spinoza's distinction between two kinds of 'power': the individual capacity of *potentia*, or 'potency', and the legislative authority of *potestas* or 'power over', later applied to contemporary politics in Hardt and Negri's *Empire* (2000). One should note that the idea of 'potentia' (as opposed to 'actus') was taken originally from Aristotle and has also been influential (since the sovereign act is one which exhausts its potentiality not to exist) in Agamben's notion (1998) of the 'sovereign ban'[19] which establishes that 'state of exception' (such as in an 'emergency') to the law that nevertheless constitutes the law and political life.[20] While Aristotle had excluded the zone of 'natural life' (confined to the household) from the zone of politics and the law, so foundationally excluding 'natural life' from Western political thought, Agamben (1998) posited that a zone of 'bare life', a politicised form of natural life, emerged from the sovereign ban in which law and fact were indistinct and which was directly subject (abandoned) to sovereign violence.

Agamben's view differed from Foucault's description of the replacement of sovereign power by disciplinary power, as an aspect of biopower, in seeing the act of sovereign exclusion – the exercise of executive power over the exception – as still fundamental to Western political thought. To some extent he was following what he sees as Walter Benjamin's revision (1969) of Carl Schmitt's original argument (1985; cf. Mouffe 1999) that sovereignty was based on an executive act of decision that could suspend the law and establish the exception to it, since Benjamin (1940, 1969) had argued that a state of emergency had already become the rule rather than the exception for the oppressed.[21] It is not hard to see a general state of abandonment or the workings of a Guantanamo-type of state terrorism (Fiskesjo 2003) in the 'war on drugs', although the relations between that global state of the divestment of rights and the extrajudicial killings that Turton and others had earlier discussed may require further adumbration.

Lash's argument (2007) for a post-hegemonic understanding of power is complex but in outline suggests that power has now become ontological rather than epistemological, or that the two have become fused in the immanence of power. There is no 'hegemon' standing above others. The idea of 'discourse' and hegemony was essentially epistemological, and power formerly achieved through symbolic representation has now moved towards a power accomplished more through forms of communicative control. Žižek had argued (with Butler & Laclau, 2000) that the resistance to the Lacanian, language-like 'symbolic' was now located in the 'real', the unutterable, the incompleteness of subjectivity (the limits of Althusserian interpellations). Lash partly agrees but posits further that domination as well as resistance are now located in the ontological 'real', and that *invention* ('performing the exceptional') has come to replace the merely negative notion of *resistance*; performance (which is what 'the communication' works through) supplants legality as a mode of legitimation. Hegemony presumes both legitimate domination and sovereignty, and both presume a dualism between ruler and ruled. US power is now well beyond the phase of hegemonic consent and alliance, he claims (against Hardt & Negri 2000); it is a matter of absolute domination, achieved through the communications order rather than through social relations. Here is where we can perhaps (not-very-finally) locate some of the past work of Turton; in *puissance* and potentia ('power to' or 'power within') rather than *pouvoir* and potestas ('power over'), and moreover in a concern with that inventiveness and creativity which may mark the limits of a domination that has now gone beyond shifting alliance and allegiance to become instituted in what Lash (2007) calls the 'vitalization' of power and the 'mediatization' of life.[22] And of course that remains an ongoing project.

Notes

1   See also Turton's essays in Hart et al. (Turton 1989a, 1989b).

2   At the end of this article I relate this interest in creative agency to theories of puissance, but it may be that these were reflected in notions of praxis theorised from Yugoslavia in the 1960s and 1970s, as a creative, committed relationship of theory with practice. From a paper given by Turton just before the conference at which this paper was first presented it became clear how important the notion of praxis has been for him. For many of these theorists, free ('good') praxis was seen as working throughout all Aristotle's three types of science: 1) theoretical, or concerned with truth, 2) poetic, concerned with making beautiful or useful things, and 3) the practical (praxis) science of politics and ethics itself.

3   However, see forthcoming doctoral thesis by Benjamin Dierikx at the Australian National University who has worked on the Thai-Cambodian border ('Life in the Margins: Local perceptions of the Thai-Cambodian border'), and Anjalee Cohen (2007).

4   On this particular issue, see David Parkin's introduction to the collection he edited (1996) with Lionel Caplan and Fisher in honour of Abner Cohen. Abner Cohen's work on cultural politics (1976, 1993) was also most influential in the SOAS Department of Anthropology where Turton worked, as this collection by their colleagues showed.

5   Gramsci. *Prison Notebooks* (1992, 1996). Gramsci is actually ambivalent about common sense, which he contrasts to 'good sense' as something which is assumed by all and may form the object of criticism – but both form a part of what he calls 'spontaneous philosophy' found in 1) language 2) common and good sense, and 3) religion and general folklore. See Nun & Cartier (1986), where the influences of Vico and Croce, William James and Bradley are considered on Gramsci. As they say, Gramsci was within a tradition that considered common sense not as negatively defined by reason but as importantly without or beyond rationality.

6   See Williams (1977, 1980). Of course the general re-evaluation of the role of culture
     and 'ideology' was an ongoing tendency associated with the Frankfurt School and, la-
     ter, the Birmingham School of Cultural Studies. The notion of 'social experiences in
     solution' (Williams 1977) has been compared and contrasted with Bourdieu's habitus,
     Foucault's episteme and Gramsci's hegemony (Filmer 2003).

7   Bloch (1985) later glossed this as 'ideology' and 'cognition'.

8   'I thought of what I wanted to say, but couldn't utter it' (Turton 1984: 67).

9   From that point of view one would have to take into account also Leach's warnings
     (1961) not to confuse the level of the 'ideal' stated by our informants with either the
     level of statistical averages (the 'norm') or the level of everyday practice ('actual beha-
     viour') or Firth's endeavours (1964) to rescue a level of 'social organisation' from the
     ideal models of 'social structure'.

10   See Brun (1987, 1990).

11   For accounts of some of these issues, see Glassman (2005); Pasuk & Baker (2004);
     McCargo & Ukrist (2005); McCargo (2006, 2007).

12   For a description and analysis of Thaksin's emergent populism, see Pasuk & Baker
     (2008).

13   This follows the context of other works by Arghiros (2001) and collections by Ruth
     McVey (2000) and Kevin Hewison (1997).

14   Yoshinori translates this as a 'paternal "father of the province"', but it sounds almost
     like a polite way of *not* saying 'jao pho' or local 'godfather'.

15   What I see as ethnomethodological is the refusal to stray outside actors' own por-
     trayals of their social situations. Indeed this can lead to a radical relativist subjecti-
     vism, which we can contrast to the views I have cited above from, for example,
     Feuchtwang and Bourdieu, Leach and Firth. Yoshinori actually refers to Goffman
     (1959), who may be regarded as a forerunner of ethnomethodology (despite his differ-
     ences from Garfinkel).

16   And this does beg the question, for in the Foucauldian notion of 'discourse' there is
     indeed no truth value outside of a highly conditioned regime of power/knowledge,
     which may be taken as paradigmatic of the post-modern 'turn'. Yoshinori refers both
     to Foucault and to Geertz.

17   The logical end of such approaches may ironically be to question the role of formal
     constitutional rule altogether, by pointing to the sort of originary violence Derrida
     (2002) discusses in relation to the notion of the 'mystical foundations of authority'
     found in Benjamin and Schmitt.

18   Thus it is ultimately ethnomethodological in accepting informant statements and ac-
     tions at face level, and eschewing the attempt at further analysis. Unlike Yoshinori,
     however, Walker does note both Turton (1984) and Scott (1976) as pointing to the im-
     portance of local political processes.

19   See also Nancy (1994) on the abandonment/banishment of Being to the law and so-
     vereign power.

20   These divisions were enormously important in scholastic philosophy, where *potentia*
     referred to potency, the aptitude to change, the determinable being rather than the de-
     termined being, and was seen as a material characteristic unlike God who was *Actus
     Purus* or perfect actuality. Any act has several potentialities; its potentiality not to exist
     is negated when/if it comes to exist. For Spinoza, however, God as Nature seems to
     have combined actuality with potentiality, while *potestas* referred to legitimate authori-
     tative earthly power or sovereignty.

21   The relationship between Schmitt, who influenced Benjamin, and the latter's own the-
     ory of a pure revolutionary violence beyond the law is complex. One might say that
     where Schmitt, for whom the state of exception and emergency were not synon-
     ymous, sought to present a form of violence as necessary and constitutive of right,

Benjamin envisaged a violence beyond the law which might transform it, if a genuine (effective) state of emergency could be brought about. See Benjamin's 'Critique of Violence' (1921, 1977) and Derrida (2002) for a discussion of it in terms of the relationship of an originary violence to the law and the difference between law-preserving and law-making violence, and Agamben (2005).

22 Vitalism as a philosophical tendency refers to a philosophy of becoming, flow, movement and organic self-organisation by contrast with mechanistic theories of causation and has been associated with Schopenhauer, Nietzsche, Bergson and Simmel. Lash discerns vitalism partly in Foucault, Deleuze & Guattari (1983) and Negri, rather than say Durkheim or Bourdieu, and argues that there has been a shift from mechanistic to vitalistic power; life is now conceived of in informational terms in a kind of neo-vitalism (Lash 2006; but cf. Ploger 2006).

6 'Modernising Subjects': Moral-Political Contests in Thailand's Drive Toward Modernity

Jamaree Chiengthong

Introduction: 'Looking at the stars with feet firmly on the ground'

In 2000, Peter Hinton commented on an important regional 1994 conference on 'cross-border' relations in Asia he had attended, which had seemed to him to be full of hope and enthusiasm. The businessman and the scholar who organised the conference were proposing an 'Asian form' of capitalist expansion. Remarking on John Naisbitt's view (1966) that networks like that of the overseas Chinese were now replacing nation-states, Hinton described this as a ludicrous attempt to combine 'the *gemeinschaft* of the traditional kinship structure' with 'the *gesellschaft* of the high technology global computer virtual society to create an invincibly dynamic machine for capitalist expansion' (2000: 13). Despite such early optimism, which Hinton criticises while allowing for the importance of national and regional differences, the Asian economic crisis was to take place in 1997. Many large business families suffered severely from the crisis, while others somehow managed to survive. In 2001 Thaksin and his party, the TRT (Thai Rak Thai), came to power with a programme to restructure a more efficient and dynamic capitalist economy, both in the urban and rural areas, and to renew such early hopes and enthusiasm for a Thai form of capitalism. Illustrating such renewed optimism and faith in material progress, there was a photograph of him looking upward and far beyond during his first campaign, pointing his finger ahead; the subtitle below said, 'Looking at the stars with feet firmly on the ground'.

In such a context of the drive towards modernisation, one may well draw comparisons with the Italian futurists in the years before the First World War, those who have been criticised as 'passionate partisans of modernity' by Berman (1990). Citing their announcement 'Comrades, we tell you now that the triumphant progress of science makes changes in humanity inevitable, changes that are hacking an abyss between those docile slaves of tradition and us free moderns who are confident in the radiant splendor of our future', Berman concludes 'There are no ambiguities here: "tradition" – all the world's traditions thrown together – simply equals docile slavery, and modernity equals freedom' (ibid. 25). But does it?

What I want to develop here are Andrew Turton's insights into the nature of conflict in Thai society, which I see as still useful today as a foundation for understanding current developments in Thai society and its 'modernising subject'. I do this by showing how a complex interplay between modernity, tradition and culture has been embedded in ideological projects and moral-political contestations.

This paper is divided into two main parts. The first comprises a review of Turton's relevance and contributions to the understanding of Thai power relations and processes of cultural and social change in terms of the actual changes that have taken place, with some reference to my own fieldwork. In the second part I consider the topic of the subject of change, and develop and elaborate further an interpretation of the 'modernising subject' project, drawing on some comparable Italian materials.

The modernity project in Thailand

The 1960s marked the initial period of 'development' in Thailand, with the implementation of the first National Economic Development Plan. This emphasized the central role of the state in the construction of basic infrastructure to facilitate the country's process of industrialisation. When Turton undertook fieldwork in Mae Sruay, some 60 kilometres from the town of Chiangrai, the Mae Sruay-Chiangrai road was still a dirt road undergoing construction. Some rich peasants, however, were already beginning to own trucks and operate transportation services for people and commodities between Mae Sruay and Chiangrai. Turton's doctoral thesis (1976b), entitled *Northern Thai Peasant Society* with the subtitle 'A case study of jural and political structures at the village level and their twentieth century transformations', revealed the growing encroachment of state power on the rural sector in the Mae Sruay area. The thesis devoted a large part to the discussion of cases where peasants had taken their disputes to court, accepting the authority of the state in the settlement of their disputes. This modern judiciary system had largely replaced local forms of traditional dispute settlement under the authority of matrilineal descent cult groups (see Turton 1972). A new consciousness of wealth and status differences had evolved; rich peasants were beginning to associate themselves with traders and petty officials, separating themselves from the poor peasants. The crucial contradiction between the 'modern' (*samai*) and the 'traditional' (*boraan*) was frequently used by the peasants themselves 'to differentiate and pass comment on the two orientations' of society (Turton 1976b: 187).

Unlike earlier scholars in anthropology and political science, who had generally described a smooth transition towards modernity and emphasized a picture of harmonious coexistence and Thai tranquility, Turton was among the first to point out the deeply conflictual nature of Thai society at that time. In his *Thailand: Roots of Conflict*, where Turton analysed 'the current situation in the Thai countryside', he pointed directly to the facts of rural differentiation and the class formation of rich peasants as against poor peasants (1978a). The state had been very tough in suppressing peasants' and students' movements. State-civil confrontations were the order of the day (see also Glassman, this volume). Yet, as we will see below, Turton did not offer a simple class analysis of this conflict.

Power relations and cultural construction; class and ideological conflicts

One of the most important contributions of Turton to the understanding of the Thai social formation was in his paper on the 'Limits of Ideological Domination' (1984), where the Gramscian concepts of consent and coercion in establishing domination were employed to analyse state-civil relations. There he noted explicitly that '... the bourgeois as a class does not effectively or adequately control this state and its apparatuses; and so far it is certainly not opposed to it *en bloc*. Nor does the state exist primarily to serve the interests of the bourgeoisie. To some extent it exists to serve the interests of the various elements which formally comprise its ruling and governing classes, among which the military are dominant' (ibid. 29). The maintenance of the ruling class's political and institutional stability was achieved through the means of 'both ideological and violently coercive forms' (ibid. 22). This concept of the 'ideological' did not imply 'fixed meanings or systems of meanings or a fixed structure or scenario, but ... processes of the formation of ideological elements, and the interaction of these processes.' 'Classes' were also not seen as 'the subjects of fixed and ascribed class ideologies' but presented as 'a field of struggle between social forces, involving not only elements of discourse but also material forces which set limits to the space of operations' (ibid. 23). In the 1973-78 period, Turton had seemed slightly hesitant about the nature of the dominant 'class'; whether it was capitalist, pre-capitalist or both (1978a: 127-129). But by 1989, when he discussed the discourse of development, he seemed certain that the dominant class constituted a new development of capitalism under the banner of national unity (1989a).

Turton (1984) also remarked that Thailand appeared to be 'characterised by greater historical continuities' (when compared with other countries in Southeast Asia) and a 'remarkable degree of overall institutional stability over the past fifty years'. This led to his other important observation on the 'weak institutional development of civil society' (ibid. 21). Moreover, he deconstructed these continuities to show instead the 'discontinuities' that were taking shape as the traditional *Sakdina* state was recharged and fused with 'the emergence of new capitalist classes' (ibid. 27).

But despite these state attempts at cultural domination, charted by Turton, counter-movements against state cultural domination also took place. One of these, of course, was the communist movement that recruited to its cause a number of students suppressed by the 1976 coup. The other important counter-movement against the state, in my own opinion, has been the 'community culture' school of thought led by the respectable and well-loved Thai scholar Chatthip Nartsupha. Chatthip founded a journal of political economy to which a number of young Thai scholars contributed articles along Marxist lines on class and relations of production. Chatthip himself made a great impact on young scholars in Thailand through two major works – *The Political Economy of Siam 1910 -1932* (co-authored with Suthy Prasartset), and *Setthakit muban thai nai adit* [Thai village economy in the past] – in which he discussed the 'destruction' of a subsistence economy by the penetration of capitalist forces. He was against any form of state domination, whether it was feudal, capitalist or 'semi-feudal, semi-capitalist'.

Yet despite such cultural and political movements against capitalism, the Thai economy continued to grow in the 1980s. The holders of state power had eventually decided to make peace with the dissidents. Many students who had gone to 'the forest' to take up arms against the government after the military coup of 1976 were 'pardoned' and allowed to return home in the early 1980s. For those people, this was a time of defeat. Even among many of those who had not gone to the countryside themselves but had sympathised with the movement, there existed a sense of loss and regret and an unfulfilled yearning for social justice remained. There had been a kind of dignity in fighting against capitalism, even though it may have been an 'impossible dream', the kind of empty fight that Don Quixote had to undertake.

The writings of the 'community culture' school, which had done so much to contribute to the continuing critique of Thai capitalism through the 1980s, were themselves strongly challenged by academics. Bowie (1988) interviewed elderly peasants in many villages in the north and consulted extensive past written records to show how very tough rural life in the past had often been, contrary to the more idyllic picture presented by members of the 'community culture' school, since peasants faced a constant risk of insufficient production which led to periodic threats of famine. This constant state of indigence was increased by the heavy taxes in rice that peasants had to pay. Yukti (1991) similarly remarked that representations of a peaceful way of life in the past were cultural constructions, a veritable 'writing of culture' achieved in part with 'techniques' of drawings of a peaceful past way of life, like a small hut under the moonlight. However, I wish to argue that one can also see the community culture school as constituting a kind of moral construction, forming an important terrain of contestation in civil society; it signifies a real and deep-rooted battle on the moral-political front. This moral-political battle, as I see it, has also been part and parcel of the process and project of the formation of the conflictual modernising subject(s) in Thailand, to which I turn below. In the 1980s the contest had been framed in terms of a 'past peaceful way of life' opposed to the capitalist rush, with the image of cooperative labour exchange (representing traditional social relations) pitted against the current realities of hired labour, as labour itself became a commodity subject to cash relations. In the contemporary situation in the 2000s, however, the moral-political issue has come to be centred more on the Buddhist virtues of modesty and frugality on the one hand, as against what is often seen as corrupt opportunistic capitalist money on the other. I expand on this below.

The new poverty

My own field research in the early 1990s also revealed the continued importance of the rural transformations that Turton had discussed earlier. Coming from an urban middle-class background, and being familiar with this 'community culture' school of thought and the charming images it presented about pre-capitalist society, I remember I was actively surprised to find economic transaction activities in the village. 'Time' also seemed very precious, even in this rural setting. Though the farmers did not work a strict nine-to-five day as in a modern office, they still had to hurry to the fields in the very early morning so much that they did not have time to cook. They bought their already cooked breakfasts from shops in the village. Apart from farming, there were also several woodcarving workshops in the village. In nearby villages, farmers commuted to town to work as construction workers and they would return home very late in the evening. I also wrote about a lady who was the owner of a woodcarving workshop in the village who dyed her hair reddish brown and looked very *than-samai* or 'modern' indeed (1996).

But while there were already elements in the village of the quick tempo of modern life, a high degree of poverty was still quite persistent. There was, for instance, an old couple who had already passed their sixties but who still had to engage in daily wage work to earn cash to buy food. There was another old man in his seventies who was still then working for wages, also to support himself. One of his daughters had just returned from a 'job' in Bangkok, and then found unskilled work in wood-carving which she alternated with casual labour in the fields at harvesting times. People had to be very mobile in order to earn a living. The other village I studied, near a forest reserve, had been quite recently settled and people were still moving in and out, engaging in all kinds of activities off-farm and on-farm, including illegal logging, in order to earn cash and sustain livelihoods. Many people in their thirties whom I talked to expressed the wish for their children to get educated so that they would have better lives and not the hard lives of farmers. (1996).

In his thesis, Turton (1976b) had already talked about how 'clock time' and 'money time' had become more intertwined into the peasant lives of the sixties, during the time of his fieldwork. But most important for him, too, was the high incidence of poverty, which was frequently talked of by the peasants. As he put it later, 'In talking about the problems of livelihood and the struggle for survival, poor farmers almost invariably refer to "the problem(s) of the market (*phanha talat*)"', above all, 'the low market price for agricultural commodities, but also the closely related problem of high prices of agricultural inputs, and of other commodities, including food, which the producers must buy for their subsistence' (1984: 35). Peasants were constantly complaining that cash was hard to find.

This transformation of rural subjects, charted by Turton and also by my own fieldwork, is truly a critical issue. The contrasts between modern life and traditional life, the rapidly changing tempo of rural life, the hard lives of the rural poor and their often expressed difficulties of finding cash, all reflect a much more general change towards commercial relations of production, and this in itself raises important issues of the *nature* of the subject of change.

The concept of 'subject'

Turton (1984) himself was much indebted to Althusserian concepts of the subject, tempered by those of Foucault. A subject, in these views, is not only a free human agent but also a product of social and cultural construction; being subjected to a certain regime of rules, regulations, values and ideology.

The strength of the Althusserian thesis lay in its concept of 'interpellation' (addressing, recruiting, emphatic intervention or even interruption), as in the recruiting poster 'Your Country Needs You' – that process of hailing whereby a patriotic and obedient social subject is produced (Turton 1984: 42; see also Tapp, this volume). However, there were aspects of the Althusserian formulation that Turton found to be too static, i.e. rather 'formal and functionalist' whereas, as he argued,

'... ideological domination, the production of forms of social consciousness, mentalities and subjectivities, may occur in any or every sphere of existence' (1984: 38). Suggesting that relations of domination were not 'univocal', Turton found Foucault's notions (1977: 27) of the flexibility of subjects and the contestation of power relations more useful. As he put it: 'The concept of the ideological is used to refer not to fixed or systematic meanings, but to the moment of the formation of consciousness in practical activity: in work, social and cultural reproduction, and in struggle' (1984: 19).

E.P.Thompson (1968) had provided an example of a more classic Marxist approach in understanding how the transformation of the subject accompanied a capitalist production system, or what Turton phrased as the 'inculcation of new patterns and ideas, norms and values, of work and consumption, ideas which can be conceptualised as being simultaneously both forces of production and ideology' (1988: 207). However, while Thompson's model of the making of the English working class was interesting in that he gave a convincing account of how modern working man had been constructed through inculcation to match the new rhythms of the capitalist demand for work, what was still lacking in much of these works was perhaps a discussion of the role of inner spiritual conflicts.

The inner spiritual conflict that took place in the Thai context was actually pointed out in Turton (1988). Now, as I will argue below, it has become even more salient. Turton turned our attention toward the fact that fleets of vans selling merchandise were marching into the villages, and that under these pressures even the *Sangha* (Buddhist monkhood) was becoming fairly secularised. Turton wrote at that time that, 'In local terms this consumerism can be criticised in the light of Buddhist values, as fostering "greed" ...' (1988: 208). Money was entering into all spheres, not only into the sphere of economic exchange. Indeed, many scholars not necessarily belonging to the community culture school now came to lament the loss of the good old days when labour had been cooperatively exchanged in rice-producing activities. It seemed clear that cash had thoroughly penetrated the traditional exchange system and was now completely destroying traditional social bonds.

The modern crisis in the Thai political situation

When Thaksin became prime minister in 2002, he implemented a major restructuring of the bureaucratic system. A system based on the CEO (chief executive officer) was introduced into the bureaucracy, wherein prompt decision-making would rest upon the executive man in charge. The government administrative system was to be managed

more efficiently to cope with rapid economic transformation. The overall aim was to run the government system as a business. On the other
hand, attention was also paid directly to rural development. A large
amount of money was spent on the health programme and on revolving
village funds. Scholarships were given for children in rural areas to
study abroad. Everywhere people were talking about the thirty baht
health-for-all programme, as well as the one million baht village revolving funds. The 'One Tambon One Product' (OTOP) development programme set out to promote sales of village-level specialised crafts products based on 'indigenous knowledge' and local skills.

Thaksin's projects injecting money into the rural areas, however,
caused alarm in some academic circles. And it was at this point that
money and materialism once again became more general issues of concern. A certain sector of the middle class began to worry that votes had
been bought through these programmes, and such alarm further
strengthened the position of the Thai Rak Thai party, and of Thaksin
himself.

Thaksin first came to power in 2001, after the 1997 financial crisis in
Thailand, when the country had run short of foreign reserves and had
to borrow from the IMF. Thaksin's famous statement that 'the IMF is
not our father' was an artful rhetorical move that provoked nationalistic
sentiments within a certain section of the population, including some
of the middle class. The very name of his political party, Thai Rak Thai
('Thai Love Thai'), could be understood as 'because we are Thai, we
have this natural love for Thai and Thai-ness'.

However, the selling of Shin Corporation – Thaksin's telecommuni-
cation company which also owned satellites under the name Thaicom –
to Temasek of Singapore was a real blow to the Thai public. Although
owned by Shin, the satellite company was a matter of national pride
and was thought of as national property. In addition, the sale involved
an astronomic amount of money (73 billion baht tax-free, or over US$2
billion at current rates).

Though Thaksin won his second term in office, with the majority of
his support gained from rural areas, there was growing dissatisfaction
with his regime. The sale of Shin to a foreign company was used as a
weapon to disprove his avowed love of the nation. In Bangkok, the People's Association for Democracy instigated protests against Thaksin, all
wearing yellow shirts; while on the other hand, Thaksin loyalists, wearing red shirts, also demonstrated in great numbers in Thaksin's support (see Keyes, this volume). Some analysts have since argued that the
situation reflected a class conflict, with the urban middle class (the yellow shirts) pitted against the rural lower class (the red shirts). The middle class was seen in such analyses as traditionalists who wanted to
hold on to power, whereas Thaksin was understood as representing the

new movement of the masses in the sense that he knew their problems and was willing to solve them.

However, I find it difficult to agree with such a simple kind of class analysis. Rather than using a rudimentary class analysis of this nature, Turton had instead much earlier employed the concept of the 'power bloc'. By this he meant a combination of groups of different power holders, employing new sets of relations of production with a different form of 'ideological domination', which he saw as a more appropriate concept for the analysis of modern Thai power structures (1984). Even though this was put forward in the quite different context of the 1980s, I still think it provides a most appropriate way in which to analyse the current crisis in Thai politics, as we will see below. What we have here is an *ideological* battle, cross-cutting class in the formation of a conflicted modern subject.

The modern project in Italy at the turn of the twentieth century: Croce and Gramsci on class and ideological formations and battles

In order to understand better the current Thai context, we may be able to learn from the historical case of Italy (a comparison explicitly made in Turton [1984] but not elaborated on there). Italy at the turn of the twentieth century was embarking on modernity accompanied by a certain crisis of the state. The north was an industrialised prosperous zone while the south still consisted of a poor agrarian sector. Even before the First World War, the ruling class was held in public contempt by some of the younger generation. Filippo Tommaso Marinetti launched the futurist movement with the Futurist Manifesto of 1909, expressing his loathing of everything old, especially political and artistic tradition, as we saw above. Yet these futurists were also passionate nationalists. At the same time, fascism began to emerge as early as 1914 under Benito Mussolini, attracting young nationalists to join for the supposed sake of the prosperity of the country. The fascists came into power in 1922 after marching into Rome in blackshirted uniforms, propagating statism, nationalism and militarism. Mussolini gained public support by instituting massive public works and building projects. During the fascist period, the liberal critic Benedetto Croce, who was to form such an important influence on Gramsci, remained anti-fascist. Partly following Croce, Gramsci believed that the use of coercive force must imply a crisis of traditional authority, and that consensus and unity had been lost:

> That aspect of the modern crisis which is bemoaned as a 'wave of materialism' is related to what is called the 'crisis of authority'.

If the ruling class has lost its consensus, that is, is no longer 'hegemonic' (*dirigente*), but only 'dominant', living by power of coercive force, this means precisely that the great masses have become detached from their traditional ideologies, and no longer believe what they used to believe, etc. The crisis consists precisely in the fact that the old is dying and the new cannot be born; in this interregnum a wide variety of morbid systems appear.[1]

Croce had felt, as Adamson (2002: 485-6) puts it, that what a transforming society of this kind needed was a 'religion of liberty', a 'teacher for the masses'. Gramsi partly agreed. Italy at that time needed, in Gramsci's words, a 'coherent, unitary, nationally diffused "conception of life and man", a "lay religion", a philosophy that has become precisely a "culture", that is, generated an ethic, a way of life, a civic and individual form of conduct ...' Gramsci had even considered this in partly religious terms. Thus he considered that 'the writer and critic Renato Serra ... had taught the people in the same way as had Saint Francis of Assisi: both knew that to make "God disappear behind syllogisms" would "kill feelings ... strangle the ardor of faith", and that the true teacher was a "humble soul, a simple spirit" who could "reanimate in each soul a divine inebriation"' (ibid. 485).[2]

Although Gramsci accepted Croce's analysis of the significance of the moral-political contest, what he felt Italy needed was a Marxist philosophy of praxis, defined as the 'absolute secularization and earthliness of thought, an absolute humanism of history'.' He saw this as '... a philosophy which is also a politics, and a politics which is also philosophy.'[3] The working class should be responsible to undertake this.

Of course for Gramsci, any class or combination of classes that aimed to establish its dominance in a society must '... stress and develop the twin moments of economic and political alliances on the one hand, and on the other, of moral and cultural appeals' (Turton & Tanabe 1984b: 5). Thailand in the 2000s has already passed the era where the use of coercive force directly supports the ruling authorities, but the ideological battle in the emerging civic sphere has now become fierce and intense, similar to the Italian case much earlier, and morality and politics have, in this new conjuncture, become closely interwoven.

The moral and cultural contest: money and frugality

The Thai anthropologist Sanit Samuckakarn borrowed the title for one of his books from a Thai proverb, *mii ngoen kau nub wa nong; mii thong kau nub wa pii*, which literally translates as 'having silver maintains the status of a younger kin; having gold will maintain the status of an older kin'. The title pointed to the significance of patron-client relations in traditional Thai society, which has always been built around a strong respect for people with wealth and power. While political scientists and earlier anthropologists such as Hanks (1962) had emphasized the importance of patron-client relations in Thai politics and social organisation, Turton had tried to point to the emergence of 'local intermediaries' who linked state power at the top with the locality at ground level. We have already noted how his 1976 thesis mentions rich peasants associating themselves with traders and petty officials. This was an accurate analysis. With the 'community development' policies initiated by the state since the 1960s, new community leaders were being created as agents of state development, and some of these became 'vote bosses' (*hua kanaen*) at election time, building social networks 'vertically from below at village levels with provincial and national politicians' (Turton 1989a: 86). Arghiros (1993), whose doctoral thesis was on politics and elections in a central Thai plain village, has discussed the ease with which Thai people can accept money as a kind of gift, at a wedding, at a funeral or at an election. In Arghiros's interpretation, money can act as a kind of social cement facilitating assistance among members in the community. Thai politicians seem to understand such patron-client relations and be able to manipulate the displays of wealth that support them. They make sure they appear in community ceremonies and donate money to ensure respect. Thaksin's rural development programmes of course involved a relatively large budget, which his public relations team ensured would be well publicized in the press. Of course, Thaksin also portrayed himself publicly as a successful rich businessman. This went well with basic Thai perceptions of money. The roof of a Thai temple is usually decorated in gold, a symbol of the wealth of the community. In the traditional *pha pa* ceremony of giving alms to the temple, which usually takes place after the period of Buddhist Lent, bank notes are displayed on small ceremonial trees so that all participants in the ceremony can admire the trees and the money that adorns them before they are donated to the temple. Displays of wealth can be used to establish social position as well as to attract followers.

Although Thais may admire money-decorated trees at the *pha pa* ceremony, I would argue that charity and modesty also remain important virtues at a more abstract spiritual level beyond this mundane display of wealth. People are also expected to be persistent in their good deeds. Bloch and Parry (1991) suggest that all societies have systems of morality sanctioning money transactions, which determine how much wealth one can expect to accumulate and distribute. Thai society is replete with examples and models of these virtues. Maha Vessandorn is one well-known example in Thailand of a 'holy soul' who did not accu-

mulate but gave away wealth in order to achieve greater spiritual en-
lightenment. The personality of Maha Vessandorn continues to represent an ideal of modesty and self-sacrifice that Thais of all classes have
been brought up with.

An account of the less well known Mahachanok, another Buddhist
figure, was translated by His Majesty the King and came into print after
the IMF incident. This gave an example of the importance of the virtues
of enduring hardship and of modesty. A cartoon version was made to
reach younger audiences. It was also famously performed on stage
when a popular young male actor played the role of Mahachanok (rather
than an actor from the Department of Fine Arts in the Ministry of Culture). And the 'self-sufficiency economy' advocated by the King was presented, in tandem with this, as a form of everyday practice in which the
virtues of frugality and modesty could be applied. With Gramsci's
words about the need for a true teacher who is a 'humble soul, a simple
spirit' in mind, we may recognise in such examples and models the importance of the fierce cultural and moral political contest between values of wealth and modesty which is now occurring in Thailand.

The 2007 modern crisis, in my view, cannot be interpreted in simple
class terms. It is much more an ideological battle that cuts across class
lines. It involves the construction of a subject who is, on the one hand,
a free agent who acts, but on the other hand is a container of certain
kinds of values, with an inner life, we may say, that can be conflicting.
In Berman's *All that is Solid Melts into Air* (1990), he shows concern
about '... the immense power of the market in modern man's inner
lives: they look to the price list for answers to questions not merely economic but metaphysical – questions of what is worthwhile, what is hon-
ourable, even what is real' (1990: 111). He adds that 'to be modern is to
live a life of paradox and contradiction. ... It is to be both revolutionary
and conservative ...' (ibid. 13).

Conclusion

I have chosen to title this paper 'Modernising Subjects' since I see the
issue of modernity as ongoing and crucial to the anthropology of Thailand; it is also crucial to understand how and in what aspects and with
what emphasis the construction of a modern Thai subject has been undertaken. From the work of Turton we saw something of how the modern subject has been constructed through state encroachment upon the
rural area, and how a patriotic social subject was produced and made to
fit with the capitalist production system, as money began to enter into
all spheres of life. Though there have been analyses of simple class conflict as a constitutive factor of political unrest in the current Thai situa-

tion, these confrontations and accommodations between modernity and tradition are multi-dimensional. In these confrontations and accommodations, ideological battles cut across class lines to involve traditional/modern values and norms, and classes may be split along vertical lines comprising 'power blocs' within factions, each contending to exert supremacy in the interpretation of cultural righteousness and to achieve ideological domination. But this is still an unfolding project in which, as Turton once said, 'norms and regulations are not yet settled'.

Notes

1	As cited in Adamson (2002: 485-86) from Gramsci (1971: 276).
2	Adamson draws on Gramsci's obituary of Serra here.
3	Ibid.

Farewell party for Turton, 1970

7 An Early Critical Foray into Participation in Thailand

Jonathan Rigg

Introduction

The term 'participation' has been problematic due to its multiple inter-pretations and because its meaning has been compromised by the iro-nic, but common, process of mainstream appropriation of a once-radical development concept. Wider debates around participation have a salience and a purchase in Thailand. In this short paper I am interested in putting these debates in context, in particular through an examina-tion of Andrew Turton's (1987) book *Production, Power and Participation in Rural Thailand: Experiences of Poor Farmers' Groups* and its relevance to subsequent applications of the term 'participation' in national devel-opment plans, critical literature and alternative development pro-grammes. I thereby wish to consider the sequel to the 'story' that Tur-ton tells in terms of Thailand's development trajectory – and in particu-lar, rural development trajectory – in the more than two decades since the book was published. The date of its publication, after all, marks the beginning of Thailand's so-styled economic 'boom' (Pasuk & Baker 1996). In essence, I seek to consider three questions in this chapter:

- How far do later debates about participation and participatory devel-opment, whether within Thailand or in wider terms, resonate with themes anticipated in Turton's work of the 1980s?
- To what extent does the Thai state's vision of participation – in the guise of the NESDB's five-year national economic and social devel-opment plans – conform with or undermine the transformative and yet materialist interpretations of participation in Turton's work?
- What reflections on participation, as it was considered in an earlier development era, does hindsight offer us through a reflection on Turton's book?

Background to the book

In the early 1980s, the United Nations Research Institute for Social De-velopment (UNRISD) established a multi-country research project that defined participation as 'the increase of control over "resources and regulative institutions" by excluded and less privileged groups' (Turton 1987: 48). The project on which Turton's book draws formed the Thailand section of this programme, and it was 'committed to a "participatory action" research style and methodology' (ibid. 4). There were six field sites: in the Sanpathong and Samoeng districts in Chiang Mai province; in the Kalasin, Udon and Yasothorn provinces in the Northeast; and in the Sanamchaiket district of Chachoengsao province in the east. The book also drew on separate work in Korat and Uthai Thani (the latter by Philip Hirsch; see Hirsch 1990).

Popular participation in Thailand

Popular participation (PP) is translated into Thai as *kan mii suan rûam khong prachachon*. The key words are *suan rûam* which mean part or share and common, mutual or sharing. Turton notes (1987: 10, fn 6) that *rûam* with a falling tone means 'to share' or 'to join in', which is closely related to *rūam* with a mid tone which is usually translated as 'to combine', 'to add', or 'to sum up' (Haas 1964). Thus we have two subtly – but importantly, given the discussion here – different intepretations. *Suan rūam* (สวนรวม) is equivalent to the English term 'the common good' or 'the public good', which Turton takes to mean 'the sum of individual interests'. But *suan rûam* (สวนร่วม) he suggests involves a 'more subjective and involuntary involvement in activity of a more of less collective nature' – i.e. participation. He also notes that at the time he was writing, the concept of popular participation was 'probably not familiar to the majority of the rural poor' (ibid. 10).

Turton (ibid. 12) reflects on how participation means different things to different people in different contexts (see Table 7.1):
– Merely creating a sense of participation
– Bridging the communication gap between the state and the people
– Improving access to resources by poor people
– Decentralisation

In noting these differences, Turton anticipates some later debates about scales (see e.g. Michener 1998; Agarwal 2001; Cornwall 2003), forms and intensities of participation. It is clear that he was aware, even in the mid-1980s, that participation was in danger of slipping through the fingers of scholars – and being co-opted by the state for its own (often non-participatory and even anti-participatory) purposes. But for Turton and the UNRISD project, participation involved the fundamental restructuring of power, and therefore control, through collective action (Turton 1987: 12). Although Turton does not use the term in the book, this is empowering, and therefore transformative.

Michener, in the context of her case study in Burkina Faso, writes of 'planner-centred' and 'people-centred' participation (1998: 2105). Planner-centred participation focuses on the need for projects and interventions to be efficient and effective; this can be aligned with Turton's types 2, 3 and 4 in Table 7.1. Participation becomes the means by which planners can increase the likelihood of success. Local people are more likely to accept development interventions and associated technologies if participation occurs. This is often the way in which multilateral organisations and, increasingly, government agencies see participation. People-centred participation, by contrast, is an end as well as a means. Radical, transformative participation is likely to be seen at the local level in the efforts of grass-roots activists – although this division is far from being a reliable one. In Table 7.1, this accords with type 5 and, perhaps, type 1.

Popular participation in National Economic and Social Development Planning

Turton (1987) notes that PP entered the mainstream planning process from the 5th Five-year plan (1982-1986). Nonetheless for the NESDB, as for the World Bank, 'participation', Turton argues, mainly means participation in the market economy. It is worth reflecting on how the terms and their meaning have changed in mainstream development discourse in Thailand. This can be achieved through the lens of the NESDB's national development plans (Table 7.2).

Table 7.1 *Linking Turton's participation types to other typologies*

	Forms of participation	Essence	Turton's critique
1.	'Merely' creating a sense of participation	(Pseudo-)participation masquerading as transformative	
2.	Bridging the communication gap between the state and the people	Instrumental – aimed at efficiency issues	This ignores the fact that the state penetrates into people's lives
3.	Improving access to resources by poor people	Nominal – focused on issues of access	Needs are historically and culturally determined and awareness arises from contest and conflict
4.	Decentralisation	Legitimation – gives the (false) impression of reallocating power and control	Often results in increasing the power of local elites
5.	Re-structuring of power through collective action	Empowering and transformative	

Table 7.2   *Participation and Thailand's national development plans (1982-2006)*

Plan	Statements and definitions regarding participation	Tenor of the plan
5th Plan (1982-1986)	'Participation' is central to the 'new' rural development strategies: 'the chief aim of the Fifth Plan is people-oriented so the rural poor will be able to help themselves' (page 278). Five salient features are identified of which #3 is 'to initiate people's self-help programmes', #4 is to 'solve problems [through] self-help techniques' and #5 is 'to encourage the maximum participation by the people' (page 278).	Focus on poor people and poor regions but in an instrumentalist manner; the plan stresses 'mobilisation'. Self-help and participation are seen as means to the achievement of the ends of development.
6th Plan (1987-1991)	In the rural development section, the plan states that the public will be encouraged to find solutions to their problems through 'self-reliance' (page 338). Popular participation is not highlighted; rather the 'participation' of the private sector (page 338-9). The plan notes that 'despite some success in promoting people's participation in rural development during the Fifth Plan period, most development efforts introduced are still at the initial stages ...' (page 344); but, the plan goes on to say, 'the private sector, on the other hand, has played an increasing role in supporting rural development activities ...' (page 344). 'The role of people's organisations and the general public in deciding how to solve their own problems and those of their communities will be encouraged, thus increasing self-reliance' (page 345).	Participation is widened beyond 'people's participation' to the participation of the people + public sector + private sector (i.e. agribusiness). Participation becomes a tripartite enterprise. The sixth plan begins the process of the commercialisation of participation in Thailand.
7th Plan (1992-1996)	The seventh plan emphasizes the promotion of QoL and better living conditions of poor people in rural areas, but sees this as best achieved through the promotion of 'entrepreneurial spirit' (page 133). 'People's organisations and the private sector, in particular, will be encouraged to participate in rural development to improve quality of life and security of income of the rural poor' (page 133). Emphasis on 'participation in national development'. People's participation (page 136) becomes an instrument to achieving basic needs.	Focus on market integration, commercialisation and commodification of rural production. The commercialisation of participation is taken one step further from the 6th Plan.

Plan	Statements and definitions regarding participation	Tenor of the plan
8th Plan (1997-2001)	Key development terms are used with abandon: decentralisation, popular participation, empowerment, fair distribution, stakeholders, people-centred, holistic, (popular) governance, NGOs, sustainable and trust. Promoting popular participation is a major sub-theme in area development (page 59) and is given its own (short) 'chapter' in Part VII of the plan on 'Managing implementation of the Eighth Plan' (pages147-8). The meaning of PP, however, is not defined and the statement that the plan will promote 'two main systems for popular participation in development activites' (page 147) indicates how PP is still viewed as an instrument for development.	Most 'participatory' plan to date – public and NGOs involved. Plan is 'people-centred' rather than 'growth-oriented' (page iv). Formulated at the height of the 'miracle'; implemented (or not) during the 'crisis'.
9th Plan (2002-2006)	The plan includes ample discussion of popular participation: 'mobilizing participation of all stakeholders in community development is a priority target' (page ix); 'alleviation of rural and urban poverty through the process of popular participation' (page ix); 'popular participation will encourage people from all walks of life to take part in the decisionmaking processes for national development' (page 26) Like the 8th Plan, the 9th Plan utilises the full range of development jargon: empowerment, sustainable development, holistic, self-reliance and grassroots (for instance); along with that can be seen as linked to the King's sufficiency economy such as: balanced, moral, spiritual, moderate, just, stable, ethical and harmonious.	The plan was prepared on the basis of a 'broad people-participation process' and guided by the King's 'sufficiency economy' – of which 'participants from every segment of society share a unanimous consent' (preliminary sections). The plan was formulated post-crisis, and reflects that crisis in its reflections on the risks of global economic integration and the attractions of stable and balanced development

Note: The 5th, 6th and 7th plans do not define 'participation'. It is used as a catch-all term. But the tone of the plans indicates that participation undergoes a progressive transformation from 'self-reliance' to 'market integration'.
Sources: NESDB national economic and social development plans (NESDB nd [a]–nd[e])

The plans never define what is meant by participation or people's participation. One can only assume the meaning from the context in which it is being used. The idea of participation is most radical, surprisingly, in the 5th Plan, where it is used as a way of boosting self-reliance and self-help. This needs to be understood, however, in the context of national economic conditions in Thailand in the early 1980s, when the plan was drawn up. Economic growth was slow and halting (see Figure 7.1), poverty was entrenched (Figures 7.1 and 7.2) and the state lacked the resources to make much difference. Successive oil price rises, a relatively stagnant economy in the context of rapid population growth, and an inefficient and overly bureaucratic state apparatus created a pessimistic outlook on the ability of the state to orchestrate development. 'At the close of the 1970s ... Thailand was experiencing serious economic problems and signs of increasing political and economic instability. ... [these] were magnified into a major crisis by the 1979-80 oil price rise' (Dixon 1999: 111). In this context, the focus on self-reliance was perhaps understandable. If the state was not in a position to make a substantive difference to people's lives, then perhaps they needed to undertake the role themselves?

The 6th (1987-1991) and 7th (1992-1996) plans show a significant shift in the meaning of participation; no longer does it mean self-reliance but rather participation in the modern, market economy

Figure 7.1   *GDP economic growth and poverty, Thailand (1962-2009)*

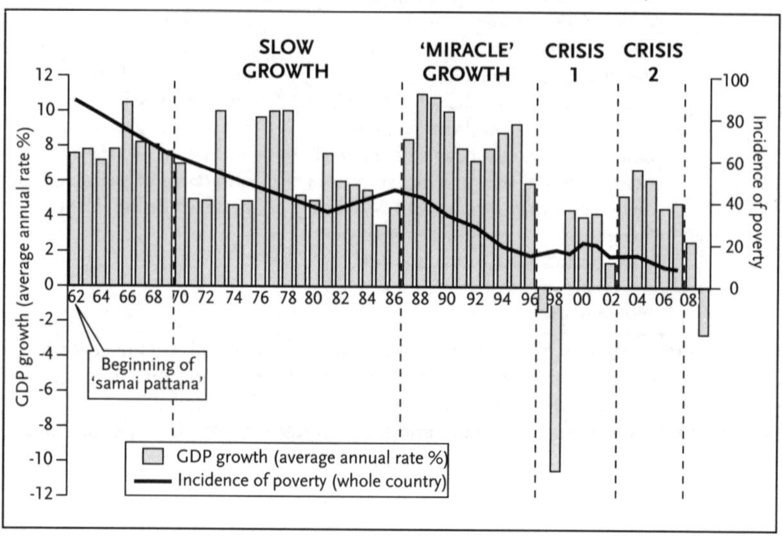

Note: This is a slightly different version of the chart used in Rigg and Salamanca (2009).
Source: UNDP 2007

Figure 7.2 *Poverty in Thailand 1975-'76, 1980-'81, 1985-'86, 1990 and 1994*

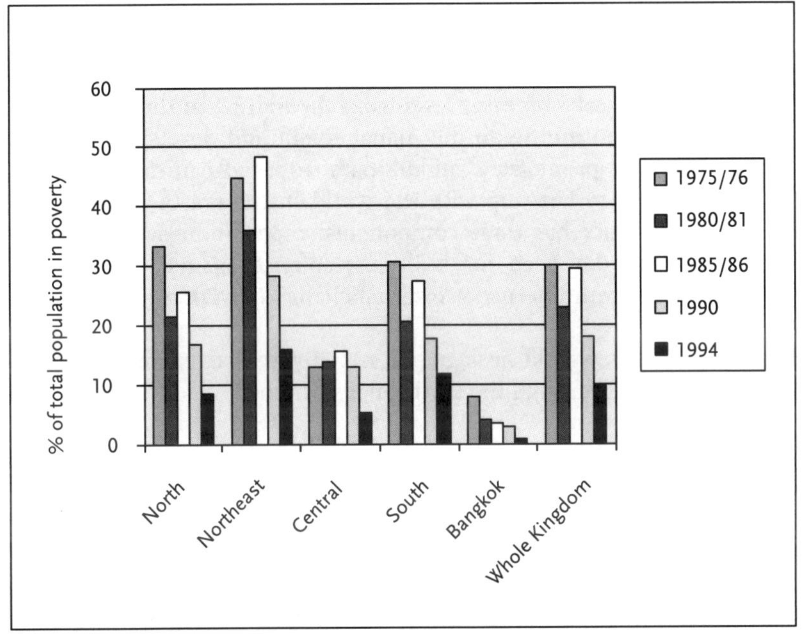

Note: These poverty data are based on Thailand's old poverty line.
Source: NESDB data from Dixon (1999: 217)

through an engagement with commerce and commercial actors. The term is the same; the context within which it is used is very – arguably profoundly – different. So, for the early 1980s, participation = self-reliance, to build (more) productive livelihoods; for the late 1980s and early 1990s, participation = market integration. It is tempting to see this shift in national plans and planning in Thailand in terms of wider debates in the institutions of the Washington Consensus, and particularly in the World Bank. Increasingly, routes out of poverty were being seen in terms of processes of market integration and incorporation.

The 8th Plan (1997-2001), formulated at the height of the Thai economic miracle, really does embrace the whole panoply of developmentally-correct terminology. The plan outlines a radical shift from 'growth orientation' to 'people-centred development', central to which was greater participation in numerous guises from political participation to involvement in community groups. But as Thailand's economic crisis was just over the horizon, the plan was effectively shelved before it could be fully implemented. The 9th Plan (2002-2006) is again very much a product of its time. Conceived in the aftermath of the economic crisis, it integrates participation with the sufficiency economy – and thereby with the King of Thailand's vision of development:

> The Sufficiency Economy is an approach to life and conduct which is applicable at every level from the individual through the family and community to the management and development of the nation. It promotes a middle path, especially in developing the economy to keep up with the world in the era of globalisation. Sufficiency has three components: moderation; wisdom or insight; and the need for built-in resilience against the risks which arise from internal or external change (UNDP 2007: 29).

Participation is now held hostage to a much wider set of meanings and objectives framed through the sufficiency economy.

Shortcomings of participation (in Thailand)

Turton (1987: 12-13) notes that in some areas of Thailand, farmers have no tradition or experience of collective action, and participation is not something that sits easily or neatly into existing structures. He also argues that 'popular participation and conflict are inseparable ... because (1) the topics of concern already contain conflicts of interest; and (2) in the (participatory) process of overcoming these conflicts ... new or more overt and occasionally heightened conflicts may be produced ...' (ibid. 14). What is distinctive in Turton's account is the way in which PP is perceived as a threat by the government and others in positions of authority. The term is seen as linked to the wider communist threat (see ibid. pp. 14-15) and considered fundamentally destabilising and therefore, from a state-perspective, threatening.

Perhaps as a result, discussion of participation in the book is used as a springboard into a discussion of grass-roots political action through rural working class movements such as the Peasants' Federation of Thailand (PFT) (Turton 1987: 35-43). What the PFT did was to establish class-based links between rural and urban producers, between peasants and workers, as well as with students and intellectuals. Participation, therefore, becomes re-framed in the book in two senses: first, popular participation becomes re-framed as the basis for a popular, and broad-based *political* movement; and second, participation becomes re-framed as a challenge to the existing structures of power in Thailand and to the elites that have dominated the country.

Considering participation in Thailand today, it is clear that this radical and de-stabilising (in a positive sense, at least for Turton) take on the approach/process no longer resonates particularly strongly. Participation, importantly without the 'popular', has become shorn of its political power and the threat it originally posed to the establishment. The fact that everyone is doing participation is part of the issue: if the Thai government, the World Bank and Asian Development Bank, NGOs and all bilateral donors are either 'doing' participation or at least strenuously encouraging it, then it is no surprise that it has lost its cutting edge and its potential to destabilise the status quo. But it is not just that everyone is doing it, and that familiarity breeds banality; one senses that the very essence of the process has been compromised. Participation has become just another method in the development tool kit, just one more instrument to achieve material ends; an empty vessel in political terms (see Ferguson 1990; Mosse 2005; Li 1999, 2005, 2007):

> Policy discourse generates mobilising metaphors ('participation', 'partnership', 'governance') whose vagueness, ambiguity and lack of conceptual precision is *required* to conceal ideological differences so as to allow compromise and the enrolment of different interests, to distribute agency and to multiply the criteria of success within project systems. (Mosse 2005: 230, original emphasis)

But while Turton is interested in power, he still takes the normative view that participation should lead to productivity increases for the rural poor (see Turton 1987: 50). In this sense, his book mirrors official documents (such as the five-year plans of the NESDB) in that participation is seen in instrumental and materialist terms (as a means to an end); it is just that Turton's means of achieving this are very different from the mainstream. That said, he argues (ibid. 72) that official development schemes with participatory elements have *not* been concerned with production. This official approach – of participation as an end in itself – could be seen, paradoxically, to be closer to how participation tends to be viewed today by activists.

So it seems to me that in the book, Turton is rather torn between the political possibilities of participation – to sideline and go beyond and behind the state (in line with Friedmann's [1992] alternative development) – and the development possibilities of the process, namely to deliver better living conditions for the poor and the marginalised. The fact that he entertains both these angles, without considering whether he is really thinking and writing about *two* participations that may be in conflict is, I think, significant.

Turton (1987) provides one example of a Farmers' Group in Yasothon in northeast Thailand that, through its size, was able to bargain collectively for better terms (such as for the prices of inputs). Participation, in this way, becomes reduced to collective bargaining power as a means of extracting greater profit/return for its members (ibid. 63). In another section of the book, participation is seen through the lens of cooperation – such as reciprocal labouring and collectively owned livestock (ibid. 67). Why this might be seen as 'participation' is not elaborated. It is noted, however, that from the perspective of the state, such collective production arrangements tend to be negatively viewed because of their communist undertones.

Participation is about the inclusion, in production terms, of the rural poor (ibid. 74). At points in the book, participation and non-participation become reframed as inclusion/exclusion (ibid. 74). Even village leaders 'are expected to participate not only in poor farmers' activities but also in official 'volunteer' activities and in community work ... (ibid. 110).

Turton does explore the ways in which community or collective decisionmaking and action are pseudo-collective: poor farmers are presented with proposals which are de facto *fait accompli* (ibid. 82). Spontaneity is limited and decisions are taken at higher levels. The system is highly bureaucratic, with only a facade of community action. Rural people are deferential and passive. When rural people are drawn into official 'participatory' structures these will tend to be, in Turton's view, 'demobilizing' (ibid. 102) rather than transformative. Turton refers to one official 'participatory' project in Uthai Thani (ibid. 104) and notes that it suffers from many of the criticisms raised earlier in the book: 'bureaucratic standardization, co-optation of village leaders, marginal, if any, relevance to local needs. It also introduces a new theme of increasing importance, namely, competitiveness'. These discussions anticipate later debates over participatory exclusions which emerged as the first wave of participation euphoria receded and some scholars and practitioners began to embrace a more critical stance on participation and the participatory process.

Reflecting on Production, Power and Participation in Rural Thailand: Experiences of Poor Farmers' Groups

Conditions in rural Thailand in the 1980s

To a significant extent, Turton bases his account of participation within the context of a particular view of the rural economy and rural society. To begin with, rural society is an agricultural society: 'It may be held to be axiomatic that production is the basis for livelihood, and that control over production is inextricably linked with control of other social resources and powers of decision-making' (Turton 1987: 48). The book tends to portray rural society as consisting of sedentary peasants, with small producers responding to the challenge of incorporation into the market economy through defensive survival strategies linked to subsistence rice production (ibid. 51, 72). Opportunities outside farming are seen to be limited to middle and rich peasants; poor farmers 'have virtually no other commercial or economic opportunities ... which might serve as sources of income ...' (ibid. 65). When farmers do engage with wider opportunities – such as working in the Middle East – this is seen only as creating a new cycle of indebtedness (ibid. 52-3). Furthermore, the integration of farmers into capitalist production is portrayed as inimical to their interests, leading to a loss of control and uncertainty. This ties in quite nicely with the more recent promotion of the sufficiency economy by activists, the Thai government (through the NESDB) and multilateral organisations such as the UNDP. So, for Turton, participation becomes a mean by which poor peasants can improve their living conditions based firmly on traditional rural activities – i.e. farming.

Multiple participations

Turton's book was published at a time when participation was in its infancy. It was also written at a time when Thailand's modernisation process appeared stalled and the country consigned, it seemed, to a long-term condition of underdevelopment. Finally, it was conceived during a period when a small farmer development ethos held sway. The participatory development paradigm being promoted by Robert Chambers, Gordon Conway and others was still regarded as radical, while in Thailand, scholars like Terry Grandstaff, who was working in Khon Kaen on various participatory initiatives, were also rather out on a limb. The Thai economic 'miracle' had yet to be recognised as such and the Thai state regarded participation as a front for (dangerous) political action. If we place *Production, Power and Participation in Rural Thailand* in this wider national and international context, then it becomes a debate-changing piece of work, at least for Thailand. What it also becomes, however, is a child of its time.

One can see, for example, that Turton does not adequately pin down the multiple (potential) meanings of 'participation'. We have in the book, participation as empowerment, participation as collective action, and participation as development. What is noteworthy – and in this sense Turton also anticipates many of the later criticisms of what participation has become – is that, notwithstanding the multiple meanings of participation in the book, the politics of action comes through very clearly.

Participation, in its original guise, was highly political: socially activist, anti-state and often anti-capitalist, participation emerged as a radical alternative to existing approaches. This is certainly the background tenor of the book (toned down, perhaps, for UN consumption). What happened, of course, is that when participation became embraced by government and mainstream development agencies, it became a technocratic and apolitical exercise. It has, one might argue, been emasculated. Chhotray, in her study of a participatory watershed development project in Andhra Pradesh (India), writes:

> In KWO's [Kurnool District Watershed Office] scheme of things, participation in the project is structured as an itemized protocol akin to the physical and financial targets of the action plan. ... KWO's protocol is essentially designed to secure the consent of village based participants, both at individual and collective levels. The centrality of consent to this entire framework rests on a liberal view of individuals as both autonomous and rational, free and willing to demonstrate their consent or, alternatively, to withhold it if necessary (2004: 343-4).

Participation has become, often, organised and structured within quite rigid protocols. Furthermore, participation is not something that emerges out of contexts of social, economic and political inequality but is regarded as something that everyone can 'do'. The politics of participation is excised from the equation, and development becomes, in the process, depoliticised. Development is no longer a struggle between classes and between local people and the state, but something that can be reduced to a simple economic activity where technical solutions are sufficient to deal with the problems that arise. This is certainly not an accusation that can be levelled at Turton's account which, like so much of his work, is combative and socially activist.

Summary

This chapter has argued, through the lens of Turton's *Production, Power and Participation*, for the importance of taking a historical perspective not only in terms of understanding contemporary conditions of development and underdevelopment, but also in terms of the lexicon of development terminology. There is, as has been noted elsewhere (see Rigg et al. 1999), a cross-cultural component to languages of development; there is also, though, an inter-temporal perspective. Turton's book, though not very widely read either in Thailand or beyond, is an important text in the context of the wider and longer debate over (popular) participation. As this short commentary has observed, in some respects it was ahead of its time – and it continues to highlight visions of participation that have resonance some two decades after it was published. It can also be used as an entry point into a debate over how development terminology becomes shaped and re-shaped over time, and sometimes 'highjacked' by powerful actors.

While Turton's book is important for the reasons outlined above, I also think – and here I must stress that this critique comes with the benefit of hindsight – there are evident gaps: the failure to define and pin down participation and what it means and entails, in particular. There is also little consideration of gender issues and wider concerns for so-called 'participatory exclusions' (see Agarwal 2001; Mosse 1994, 2001; Resurreccion et al. 2004). Indeed, the politics of rural Thailand at this time seems to push gender out of the frame, in favour of a class-based analysis. In addition, there is a tendency to essentialise rural Thai society, or at least the peasant part of it. 'Poor farmers' are represented as an undifferentiated group. In the early 1980s this might have (just) still been largely true, although I doubt it; today, of course, participation occurs in a context of considerable rural differentiation.

8 Thai Institutions of Slavery: Their Economic and Cultural Setting

Craig J. Reynolds

One of the many values of revisiting the work of a senior scholar is that we have a chance to consider the political and social circumstances of the historical moment in which the research was originally conducted and written up. This exercise may bring to light ideas and insights that have new significance in this contemporary moment. Too often, it seems to me, citations to important research refer merely to little known facts or details and fail to take account of the overall impact of the research, or how it has subsequently developed. For reasons I do not entirely understand, subsequent work on the same topic may neglect to mention earlier studies that have put their stamp on the topic or charted new courses in the field. This is certainly the case with Andrew Turton's article 'Thai Institutions of Slavery', published in 1980 in a volume on Asian and African systems of slavery (Turton 1980).[1] For a teacher of modern Thai history, Turton's analysis is the work of choice for beginning and advanced students about these institutions of bondage that affected political, social, economic and financial life in pre-modern Thai society.[2] In the following discussion, I will place Turton's study of slavery in a broad context and assess its impact on subsequent work. Moreover, as I am going to suggest in my conclusion, aspects of Thai institutions of slavery are very much alive today, despite the much-heralded emancipation of Thai slaves between 1874 and 1905 by the fifth Bangkok king.

Turton's 'Thai Institutions of Slavery'

What does Turton say in 'Thai Institutions of Slavery?' The essay is lengthy partly because Turton is so scrupulous about drawing into the discussion previous classics in this field. For Southeast Asia, Bruno Lasker's comparative study in 1950 is one such foundation text, and for Thailand the work of Robert Lingat (1931), a French legal scholar and adviser to the Thai government, is another. After a succinct account of pre-modern Thai history, Turton gets down to business by discussing different categories of slaves and different types of servitude and bondage, hence the plural noun in the title, *institutions*.

There were war slaves, combatants who were pressed into slavery following their capture and sometimes given to nobles as gifts, thereby serving as a form of currency in political transactions. Wars seem to have been little more than slave raids, a routine exercise during the dry season. The numbers involved could be huge. When they took Vientiane in 1826, the Siamese captured some six thousand families and relocated them to the central plains. In the late thirteenth century the wife of King Mangrai brought five hundred slave families as part of her dowry, and later in the small Lannathai kingdom many thousands of slaves were said to be owned by the aristocracy, contributing protection as bodyguards and serving as retinues that signified royal or noble rank (Turton 1980: 255-256; 275). Katherine Bowie is even more emphatic on this point for northern Thailand, arguing that at least half of the population were war captives (1996: 105). Turton himself recently returned to the theme of violence in the acquisition of people for exchange in an essay showing the similarities between state-centred Tai slaving raids and those of the Karen (2004).

In addition to war captives, there were also monastery slaves. These were individuals or entire families donated to monastic establishments for the cultivation of land and the care and upkeep of the monastery and its inhabitants. In frontier regions these labour endowments to monasteries (*lek phra; kha phra yom song*) facilitated new settlements and the expansion of the kingdom (Turton 1980: 259; Reynolds 1979). Judicial slaves were those punished for a crime and condemned to servile status and hard labour for the extent of their natural lives and sometimes of their descendents (Turton 1980: 261). In addition to these types of slaves, there was an active slave trade that brought upland minority peoples into the lowland states. The hill people were valued for their 'uprightness' and, lacking kinsmen in close proximity, were prized because they were less likely to escape. While slave raids were often inter-ethnic, it seems traders on occasion were quite capable of acquiring people from their own ethnic group as slaves for exchange (ibid. 257-258).

Turton's account proposes that an important change took place around the beginning of the nineteenth century. Slaves in all categories gradually became 'slaves by purchase', meaning that they could potentially be redeemed if someone was willing to pay out their price or extinguish their debt. He discusses at some length, and intermittently throughout the rest of the essay, 'debt slaves' or 'debt bondsmen', which have been studied extensively by historians of India where agricultural labour was indentured and became the object of British scrutiny and reform (Prakash 1990). People were used as collateral, and were in effect mortgaged against debts. In Siam during the first half of the nineteenth century, 'the overwhelming majority of slaves' (*that*) was redeemable.

They were *that* as a result of indebtedness. The number of such slaves was increasing – largely, according to many commentators including Akin (1969), because they willingly sold themselves into the condition. Akin's 1969 study had given ample evidence of free persons, or *phrai*, especially *phrai luang* or king's *phrai*, who preferred servitude as *that* rather than submit to the corvée obligation or to the harsh treatment of a cruel master.

This line of argument leads Turton to assess the extent of cruelty and abuse as best he can, given the scanty evidence available about the actual conditions in which slaves lived.[3] Generally he advances the view, correct in my opinion, that while it is important to understand the local nuances of *that* in the context of Thai social organisation, slavery (*kanpenthat*) was 'a form of bondage in which human beings are a form of property', as Barry Hindess and Paul Hirst would put it. Because they were a form of property, they could be treated as chattel. Jit Poumisak pointed out that the word for 'lord' and for 'owner' in Thai was, and is, the same word, *jao*. Turton cites Hindess and Hirst again to demonstrate that the master of the slave is the slave's owner, not the slave's lord. Extending Turton's line of thought, one can see that the Thai language fuzzied up this difference in a clear case of what Marxists used to call accusingly, and often too gleefully, mystification (Turton 1980: 264). In a critical essay clearly informed by Turton's work, Bowie, whose evidence is based on archival sources and oral accounts in northern Thailand, also challenged the benign portrayal of Thai institutions of slavery by envoys, travellers and academics. She tracked down a legacy of complacency beginning with the nineteenth-century accounts of Bishop Pallegoix, Sir John Bowring and Archibald Colquhoun and continuing through the academic studies of Akin (1969), James Ingram (1971) and R. B. Cruikshank (1975) and argued that more people were enslaved by physical force than by economic circumstances (1996: 131).

One of Turton's conclusions, which helps to illuminate the role of slaves in Thai society, is that slaves did not constitute a distinctive socio-economic class. They tended to be found in the less productive aspects of the economy, but no labour process was exclusive to slaves. Although he found no slaves engaged in mining or administration, they were employed in craft production of all kinds, domestic service and any other kind of service such as the owner (*nai*) might require, and sometimes in public works (building fortifications, canals and roads) and as bodyguards and soldiers (1980: 278, 281-282).[4] Some of these tasks were also performed by free persons, especially *phrai luang* but also by wage labourers as the nineteenth century proceeded. He confronts the question of whether Thai slaves were employed in agriculture and advances the idea, more by hypothesis than by empirical verification, that 'some slaves were engaged in agricultural production', in which he includes irrigation, the maintenance of paddy fields and the production of livestock (ibid. 278). His argument here seems to be that if the agricultural economy is envisioned in a comprehensive way, slavery was indirectly used for agricultural production. While there has been debate on this point, in fact, most Thai and Western economic historians seem to agree that slaves were rarely used in agriculture, and if they were so used, only on a small scale (Brummelhuis 2005: 43). Only in the Rangsit irrigation scheme that developed north of Bangkok at the end of the nineteenth century were slaves under the control of aristocratic landowners used for rice cultivation (Sunthari 1987). Overall, he stresses that the difference between slaves and other types of labour is that *that* were 'regarded not merely as an inferior, unfree human subject, but even to some extent as less than fully human' (Turton 1980: 288).

Another conclusion that should be highlighted at this point is that it was not the productive capacity of Thai *that* that was important in premodern times and through the late nineteenth century. Rather, it was the significance of slaves as indicative of wealth and status, an asset that could be displayed in retinues and entourages. Slaves were assets that signified prestige; they were visible signs of wealth and power. When a dignitary moved, 'every emblem of rank and office (sword, betel boxes, cushions, fans, etc.)' accompanied the person, requiring the labour of the servile classes. Slaves were producers of a mode of consumption that the noble and royal families sought to monopolise and display for maximum effect to express their status as the ruling class (*phu phokkhrong* in Thai). Social scientists writing in the wake of Turton have taken up this point, noting that value in the Siamese world was not determined exclusively by economic scarcity and economic utility (Brummelhuis 2005: 41).

A particular strength of Turton's account, and here his anthropological training gives him advantages that historians do not necessarily enjoy, is his observation that the Thai bilateral kinship system afforded 'ease of entry or committal into slavery by persons of both sexes' (1980: 273-4). Because of the bilateral system, slaves were more easily assimilated into new communities or into their owner's households without stigma than would be the case in unilineal systems such as the Chinese. James Watson, the editor of the book in which Turton's essay appeared, proposed a distinction between 'open' and 'closed' systems of slavery, the Thai case being an instance of the former. This distinction was picked up subsequently by both anthropologists and historians and now seems to be conventional wisdom (Evans 1993: 218-219; Reid 1983a).

Another strength of Turton's analysis is that the anthropologist is more aware than the historian of the extent to which one must speak of

'Tai [as opposed to Thai] institutions of slavery.' Partly this stems from the nature of his source material, which includes French and British nineteenth-century accounts of the region beyond the present-day borders of the Thai nation-state, and partly it stems from his general understanding of the highland-lowland, dominant-subordinate relations and ethnic dynamics that characterise northern mainland Southeast Asia and southern China. Turton's understanding of social identity in Tai states is on display in the 2000 volume he edited, *Civility and Savagery* (cf. Reynolds 2003).

Finally, in considering how Turton approaches 'Thai institutions of slavery', it might be helpful to note that in the Thai language, *that* is sometimes translated with inverted commas as 'slavery'. The punctuation around the term points to the lack of equivalence of *that* with slavery and implies that the Thai institution should not really be considered slavery in all respects. Perhaps we should simply refer to *that* as 'unfree labour'. Turton quotes Akin (1969), who echoes Bowring and others in saying that, 'the necessity to use the word 'slave' for *that* is very unfortunate.' Writing about forms of debt bondage in the following reign, King Vajiravudh argues that Thai forms of slavery were 'lighter' (*bao* is the Thai word here, indicating freer, less coercive) than was the case with slavery in the southern American states, another instance of the institution being cast in a benign light (Vajiravudh 1951: 54; Bowie 1996). It needs to be recalled in this context that servitude as a general category is the product of a post-Enlightenment 'discourse that discovered humanity, and liberty as the essence of humanity' (Prakash 1993: 143). This line of thinking suggests that we need to be careful in applying modern understandings of freedom and servitude to earlier times. Turton argues that insisting too strongly on the cultural specificity of Thai slavery, which is a slightly different point, renders more difficult the comparative study of slavery in Tai and other contexts, including the European one. The 'theory' of slavery is also more difficult to apply if *that* cannot be translated as slavery (Turton 1980: 263-264). Moreover, the evidence suggests that the Siamese elite in the decades of the late nineteenth century – when the institution was being critically assessed – certainly had no problems understanding the equivalence of *that* and slavery, whatever the variations in degrees of freedom and room for negotiation and dispensation that existed, particularly in pre-modern times (Brummelhuis 2005: 44).

Why did Turton publish his piece on slavery in 1980? The simple answer is that he was invited to contribute to the volume by Watson, the editor, but there were also other factors that moved him in this direction. For one thing, he worked on slavery in what I would call his 'red' period in the late 1970s through the mid-1980s. After hearing him give a very spirited talk on 'praxis' in Chiang Mai in January 2008, I am not certain he has emerged from his 'red' period. In any case, although he almost certainly was not a card-carrying member of any extreme left political party, the marks of Marx in terms of frameworks of analysis, approach and vocabulary are evident in his work at this time. In 1978 when he reviewed the political programme of the Peasants Federation of Thailand in his 'Current Situation in the Thai Countryside', Turton talked about 'contradictions' in Thai society (see Jamaree, this volume). He analysed the peasantry and other groups, such as the new rural capitalists, as a class (1978a). He took the Socialist Party and the Communist Party of Thailand seriously and related the agrarian policies of these parties to the contemporary historical moment, thus laying the groundwork for a history of radical agrarian activism in Thailand during the heyday that has yet to be written.[5] Personally, I found 'Current Situation in the Thai Countryside' a breath of fresh air, because by the time it was published in 1978, it was clear that American social scientists, particularly the political scientists, had lost their way with Thailand, having failed to acknowledge – let alone study – the dramatic economic and social changes that had been taking place since the 1950s.

In 'Thai Institutions of Slavery', Turton speaks unselfconsciously of relations of production and the social formation and several times cites the influential work of Hindess and Hirst, *Pre-capitalist Modes of Production* (1975), the bible of radical social scientists at that time. He does his best to assess the extent of coercion and violence in the treatment of slaves, and he gives the reader his judgement on whether or not a distinctive socio-economic class of slaves existed in Thai society. He pays his respect to the British Marxist historian, Perry Anderson, and he is familiar with Jit Poumisak, one of the two most astute Marxist historians of Thailand, who wrote 'The Real Face of Thai Feudalism Today' (Reynolds & Hong 1983). At the time Turton was writing, Marxist vocabulary and frameworks of analysis were second nature to many academic authors, similar to the way the vocabulary and frameworks of analysis of Michel Foucault have inflected academic discourse today.[6] However, Turton cannot be accused of crude Marxism; unlike Jit, he does not come close to finding a slave mode of production in Thai history. Towards the end of his 'red' period in 1984, these tendencies became even more pronounced in his work. He was much taken by Althusser, Maurice Bloch and Gramsci, and published 'Limits of Ideological Domination and the Formation of Social Consciousness' (1984). Although the article contains a little too much Althusser, Bloch and Gramsci at an abstract level, this introduction to the Osaka volume is certainly required reading for anyone trying to understand the way socio-economic change in Thailand allowed new hegemonies to build which are still visible in Thailand today.

Subsequent studies of Thai slavery

In a way, the appearance of Turton's 'Thai Institutions of Slavery' and other works on Thai slavery that followed in its wake was predictable. Fundamental research on American slavery in the 1960s and 1970s had turned academic attention to the African slave trade across the Atlantic and to the meaning, and especially the economics, of slavery in all societies in which it is found. The volume edited by Watson emerged in the long afterglow of Fogel and Engerman's *Time on the Cross* (1974), which itself followed on the heels of work by David Brion Davis, Eugene Genovese and others on American institutions of slavery (Davis 1967; Genovese 1969). Anthropologists, sociologists and historians such as Orlando Patterson in *Of Human Bondage, Slavery and Social Death: A Comparative Study* (1982) were keenly studying slavery comparatively.[7] The little cluster of studies on Thai slavery must be seen as a niche in this larger historiography of slavery, bondage and dependency. Terwiel's essays (1983, 1984) and the University of Michigan thesis by Chatchai Panananon (1982) all fall within the decade after the publication of *Time on the Cross*.

Of the studies of Thai slavery that followed Turton's essay and built on his research, by far the most detailed and well-documented is Chatchai's thesis, which took account of the Thai archival material in a way that Turton's essay did not. As a historian, Chatchai also dealt more thoroughly and patiently than Turton did with the dissolution of slavery as a formal, legal and therefore legitimate institution until its abolition in the last third of the nineteenth century. The story of the dissolution of the corvée system takes a similar trajectory, 'hovering' by the end of Mongkut's reign between forced labour and the poll tax (Terwiel 1984: 31). King Chulalongkorn's first decree announcing the gradual abolition was issued in 1874 around the time of the so-called Front Palace crisis, which is usually seen as evidence of the nobility's resistance to the emerging power of the king and his numerous talented younger brothers. It was clear that as he prepared to dissolve the institution, the king was striking at one of the material assets of his political opponents, the large number of people in servitude who were a visible sign of power, status and wealth in Thai society.

It took thirty years, or longer if one considers slavery in the provinces, before the institution was formally and legally extinguished. Land became a more valuable asset than people with the expansion of rice production as a result of the Bowring Treaty provisions, the construction of the Suez Canal and the international commerce stimulated by Western colonialism in the region. The value of people as a material asset declined in favour of land, and it became more socially and economically advantageous to be a peasant than a slave in the emerging economy. Labour power was thus drawn away from institutions of bondage by the rapidly rising value of land (Chatchai 1982: ch. 7).

The other major study in English to account for the abolition of institutions of slavery is by the economic historian, David Feeny, in his 'The Demise of Corvée and Slavery in Thailand, 1782-1913' (1993), which appeared in a volume more deliberately concerned with emancipation, and with the end of institutions of slavery, than Watson's 1980 edited collection.[8] More or less in keeping with the drift of scholarly opinion on the Thai case that stresses Chulalongkorn's humanitarian principles, Feeny proposes that 'domestic and international motives rather than economic incentives appeared to have played the most direct role' in ending institutions of slavery in Thailand (1993: 100). While Feeny does acknowledge that the 'domestic acceptability of the gradual abolition of slavery was enhanced by economic change' (ibid. 99), this conclusion strikes me as surprising coming from an economic historian, especially one who adeptly makes use of Chatchai's argument that the rice boom and the rising value of land undercut the economic grounds for the relations of servitude we are calling slavery. Other social scientists have concluded that bonded labour or slavery-like relations had simply become unprofitable (Brummelhuis 2005: 64). Feeny himself acknowledges that the change in property rights in human beings over the period occurred during rapid commercialisation (1989: 287). As the Thai legal system was reformed in response to pressures from the Western imperialist powers, it became more and more difficult to enforce property rights in human beings that upheld Thai institutions of bondage and servitude.

Future prospects for research

How might the complexity of Thai institutions of slavery, upheld by political, social, economic, legal factors and even moral principles, be rethought? What is the state of the field now, and where might new lines of inquiry take us?

On the very eve of issuing the edict abolishing slavery in 1905, King Chulalongkorn appeared to acknowledge that while the buying and selling of *that* had ceased to exist, the practice of giving wages to workers in advance was, in effect, a new kind of servitude that perpetuated bondage in a different form. The king apparently did not object to this practice, raising the possibility that his humanitarianism in seeking the end of Thai institutions of slavery was governed as much by *realpolitik* with respect to Western imperial pressures as by moral vision. Siam's status as an independent kingdom was 'qualified' as a consequence of these pressures, a split domain in which the sovereign agent was both colonised and coloniser (Loos 2006: ch. 1). The British everywhere in their empire were known for exerting diplomatic pressure for the suppression of the slave trade, as they did in the Ottoman world earlier in the nineteenth century (Toledano 1993: 39). They abolished slavery in India in 1843, and one suspects that they made their views on this issue known to King Chulalongkorn.

It would be interesting to know more precisely what was being said to the Siamese elite through the decades of most intense pressure, and just how these people were reacting to British attitudes towards Thai institutions of slavery. I have seen no study of the Thai case that has taken full account of British anti-slavery policies, or the French for that matter. Chatchai has a few pages on the matter with respect to the French, and he does begin to ask questions with respect to the British in terms of Chulalongkorn's own thinking (1982: 266-267, 219). Surely there is material from the British and French archives that would tell us more. Siam was forced to make a number of adjustments, such as abolishing slavery, if it was to extricate itself from the extraterritorial treaties and regain its sovereignty, but the source material for this conclusion has been raked over many times and is now threadbare (Feeny 1989: 295). It is time to revisit the topic anew with fresh eyes and newly discovered documents.

Chatchai (1982: 268) perceptively identifies the practice of advancing wages on labour yet to be completed as 'a form of slavery in disguise', a practice that ran parallel to and eventually superseded the formal institutions of slavery that were being phased out in the 1890s. Even after thirty years of gradualism in the abolition of slavery, the new accounting systems for keeping track of people through censuses, identity cards and certificates of citizenship, as well as the mechanisms for raising levies, such as the military conscription act of 1905 that emerged in the early twentieth century, did not spell the end of slavery in disguise. Debt bondage continued in various forms through the following decades. Vajiravudh (r. 1910-1925), Chulalongkorn's son and successor, discussed the practice of purchasing young women as mistresses, a cause for public concern because of the vulnerability of the women and the abuse that sometimes resulted. Vajiravudh wrote in great detail about the practice, citing a price of about 400 baht for a young woman paid through a broker, which could be bargained down if the woman was an orphan or her family were indigent.[9]

Nowadays, about a century hence, the dynamic economies emerging in East Asia and northern mainland Southeast Asia – as well as the 'closed' economies of countries such as Burma/Myanmar – are creating new imbalances in value, which in turn stimulate flows of goods and, of special interest to us here, people. As a result, the long durée of debt servitude in northern Southeast Asia, which Turton documented from the early nineteenth century, has yet to run its course. Indeed, in the amended version of his essay published in 1998 in a French volume, Turton brings up the export of coerced labour from Southeast Asia. He suggests that while the long durée might be investigated, the circumstances of neo-slavery might be 'quite specific to a new historical conjuncture' (1998: 441).

I am not in bibliographic control of all the recent work done in this field, and I might not be informed of important research that bears on this issue. But there is enough news in the international media and film documentaries about trafficking in human beings to suggest that many of the people being moved around the world nowadays are bound by debt to gangsters, people smugglers and brothel owners. That is to say, the 'owner' of a person has paid a sum of money against future wages to a family member, such as a parent, or to a previous creditor, in exchange for the rights to that person's labour. The lump sum may pay for passage across national borders and a 'package' that includes work, room and board, sometimes under coercive and abusive conditions. The interest on the principal advanced to initiate the transaction accumulates so rapidly that the indentured person has little chance of paying off the loan and is effectively bound in servitude indefinitely. Children and women, and the poor more generally, are particularly vulnerable to this kind of debt servitude. The call by Grant Evans fifteen years ago (1993: 220) for ethnographic research on debt servitude may not have been answered simply because the conditions in which such research is undertaken are violent and personally dangerous for the ethnographer. What creditor who owns property rights in human beings, now illegal in most countries, is going to hospitably open the door to a visiting anthropologist to inspect ledgers containing details about costs, dates of transactions and terms of contracts? I say 'ledgers' figuratively, as there may be no written records of these transactions.

One of the curious things about the scholarship on slavery is the way historians, anthropologists and sociologists are invited into a comparative project to write about a specific society. The editor brings to bear his or her wealth of knowledge and experience on the comparative context and writes an illuminating introduction that is quoted for years to come. But the individual essays on each society are almost never really comparative, however much they might have been informed by the other essays in the volume. Authors stick to the terrain they know best, and it is left to the reader to make the connections and comparisons across time and place, a formidable task considering the complexity of the case studies. This is a feature of edited volumes on many topics, and it is a feature of the three volumes on institutions of slavery edited by Watson (1980), Reid (1983b) and Klein (1993) cited here.

Debt bondage is a case in point, for it occurred – and still occurs – in many parts of the region, as does forced labour. To take just one example, an economic historian, Dharma Kumar, has said of India:

> In some cases, so-called debt bondage may have been a cloak for a hereditary relationship not based on a loan, but debt bondage in its true sense was found all over India and not just in agriculture. Men, and more rarely women, contracted a loan without security, frequently on the occasion of their marriage, and their labour was mortgaged until they repaid the loan. Since their wages were extremely low, they were frequently unable to do so. Parents could also mortgage the labour of their children against a loan, as parents doubtless do today, not only in India. (1993: 121)

The relevance of the Indian case, even when all the obvious differences such as caste and colonial history are taken into account, is that British anti-slavery sentiment and policy had a great impact in colonial India through the application of law to the institutions of slavery, which the British eventually abolished in 1843.

Even in Australia, debt bondage has been an issue in recent years as women have been found in sexual servitude. In May 2008 the Australian High Court heard a case in which five Thai prostitutes were forced into brothel work to repay an AU$40,000 debt before they received any wages.[10] Debt bondage had not been eradicated. It is an effect of the contemporary globalising world that deserves fresh scholarly attention from historians and social scientists.

Notes

1   Surprisingly, neither of the two articles written by Terwiel in 1983 and 1984 cites Turton's comprehensive and illuminating analysis, nor does Chatchai 1982. Turton's essay was reprinted with some minor and some significant amendments in Condominas et al. 1998.

2   I am not the only historian who notes the value of this work. For their discussion of Thai slavery, Baker and Pasuk cite Turton's essay as the standard reference on servitude and unfree labour (Baker & Pasuk 2005: 42, n25).

3   Turton does not provide many examples of abuse, but other historians of the institutions of slavery have found several cases using archival evidence; see Chatchai 1982 and the essay on Thai social history in Reynolds 2007: 72-77.

4   Subsequently, he found evidence of *that* in gold mining along the Maeklong River, and he reported this in the slightly revised edition of the paper (Condominas 1998: n4).

5   I say this notwithstanding Bruce Missingham's fine study on the Assembly of the Poor (2003).

6   Some would say 'infected'. This was true for Thailand too. When the Chiang Mai anthropologist, Anan Ganjanapan, a contributor to this volume, returned from Thailand after his Cornell PhD (1984), his own doctoral dissertation steeped in economic anthropology, he found the Thai academic world rife with Marxist debates (conversation with Anan Ganjanapan, Chiang Mai, 11 September 2007). See also Reynolds & Hong (1983).
7   See the review by David Brion Davis of Patterson 1982 in the *New York Review of Books* 30.2 (17 Feb 1983), 19-22.
8   The book, edited by Martin Klein, began life at a conference of economic historians in Budapest in 1982 and was only published eleven years later; see Klein 1993.
9   'On the Trade in Young Women' appears in one of Vajiravudh's civilizational treatises, 'Clogs on Our Wheels', first published in English in 1915, later in Thai (Vajiravudh 1951).
10 See Australian Broadcasting Corporation's Law Report on Radio National for 13 May 2008, available at www.abc.net.au/rn/lawreport/stories/2008/2241462.htm.

9   British Diplomatic Missions to Tai States in the Early Modern Period: A Reappraisal

Volker Grabowsky

Introduction

On 21 January 1830, a unique cross-cultural encounter took place in the small town of Lamphun, situated twenty miles to the south of Chiang Mai. A 33-year-old Anglo-Scottish army doctor, David Richardson, accompanied by some three dozen traders from Moulmein as well as five Indian soldiers, was received at an audience by the local ruler, Cao Luang Nòi In. This was the first encounter in over two centuries of a European with a Tai prince in the heartland of mainland Southeast Asia. In the next ten years, Richardson revisited the Tai speaking areas in present-day northern Thailand ('Siamese Shan') several more times and, in 1839, even had an audience with King Rama III in Bangkok. When Richardson started his fourth mission in mid-December 1836, he was accompanied by another young Anglo-Scot, Lieutenant William Couperous McLeod, who was three years his junior. Two weeks later, the group split up. Whereas Richardson took a northern route through the much-feared Karenni region, making his way to the Shan areas on the west bank of the Salween and from there to Ava, McLeod's group travelled to Chiang Mai and from there to Chiang Tung and Chiang Rung where no European had been before (Grabowsky & Turton 2003).

Since the 1950s, Richardson and McLeod's travel diaries or journals – most of which had remained unpublished – were rediscovered by a number of Western and a few Southeast Asian scholars for their academic research. Ma Thaung (1954) and Dorothy Woodman (1962) were the pioneers using the journals for British interest in trans-Burma trade. Other scholars drew on the journals to study such diverse subjects as politics, economy and society of Tai states, Tai-Karen relations, forced population movements in nineteenth-century Lan Na, or British colonial history. Nigel Brailey (1968) made extensive use of the journals in his endeavour to reconstruct the political dynamics in Chiang Mai before its integration into the Siamese state, and Andrew Turton (1980, 1998b) used the material as a source on Tai practices of slavery. It was Turton who years later discovered its significance for opening up a new field of research in Thai Studies, which he ingeniously called 'ethnography of embassy'. In October 1996, he first presented the theoretical frame of his then still ongoing research to a wider audience in one of the three 'special lectures' delivered at the Sixth International Conference on Thai Studies in Chiang Mai (a slightly revised version of the conference paper was published in 1997).

In this article I first provide an account of how Turton developed the concept of 'ethnography of embassy' and how my own research interests as a historian coalesced with his anthropological approach to this field. Then I discuss from a wider historical perspective how the field has developed more generally.

Ethnography of embassy

What does Turton mean by 'ethnography of embassy'? First of all, in the early modern period, which came to an end in Southeast Asia only around the middle of the nineteenth century, permanent missions of European powers in Asian countries were still a rare exception. The missions of that period were rather 'travelling embassies' and given their particular context, extraordinary kinds of transcultural encounters (Turton 1997: 178; cf. Pratt 1992; Schwartz 1994). Turton strongly emphasizes that these particular diplomatic encounters constitute a contested zone, as both sides – the early modern *farang* diplomat-explorer as well as his Tai hosts – shared the mutual interest of acquiring firsthand knowledge from one another. The accounts of both sides thus reflect 'a kind of robust honesty about self-interested purpose and difficulties of "translation" in various senses' (ibid.). When Turton speaks of 'embassy', he uses the word in a very broad sense, defining it as 'one discursive entity, extending from the inception of the mission at home, to post-mission commentaries and publications'. In a sense, the whole time spent in Tai territory might appear 'as a single ceremony, containing the focused ritual of royal diplomatic audience' (ibid. 179).

Central to Turton's methodology is the identification of recurrent themes or tropes, rhetorical figures of speech, which appear in the accounts of the travelling embassies. These *topoi* comprise, on the one hand, tropes in European perceptions of Tai diplomatic practice such as complaints about excessive ceremony and protocol, unnecessary delays or unwarranted control and surveillance. The tropes in Tai perceptions of European diplomatic practice, on the other hand, focus on fears of spying or even invasion and conquest, or highlight unusual behaviours and manners that were often considered rude. Finally, a recurrent theme that points at mutual perceptions of Western (*farang*) guest and Tai host is friendship. Not unlike the Chinese diplomatic practice of 'cherishing men from afar' that Hevia (1995) discusses in his *Qing Guest Ritual and the Macartney Embassy of 1793* (Turton has studied this groundbreaking work carefully), the Tai rulers developed an elaborate system of treating foreign guests with cordiality and friendliness. Friendship and general goodwill were also criteria by which Richardson, McLeod and others judged the success or failure of their missions. However, European perceptions and expectations of 'friendship' differed from what their Tai counterparts labelled *ratchamaitri* (royal friendship or state-to-state relations) or *maitricit* (friendliness), giving rise to occasional suspicion of the other side's sincerity (Turton 1997: 196).

Turton's concept of 'ethnology of embassy' became more elaborate when, in early 1998, he embarked on a study of the journals of McLeod and Richardson's 1837 diplomatic missions to Tai states in more depth. That was the moment when Turton's and my research interests crossed each other. My familiarity with the journals goes back to 1990 when I began my post-doctoral research on the political, social and population history of northern Thailand in the late eighteenth and early nineteenth centuries. On reading the original text, I was impressed by the wealth of information about Lan Na society (especially in McLeod's journal) during a period when the area of present-day Thailand's upper north still consisted of largely autonomous and semi-independent states. In 1995, I sent copies of the journals to Saraswadee Ongsakul, a leading scholar of Lan Na history at Chiang Mai University, who recognised their originality and brought them to the attention of Winai Pongsripian, a historian at Silpakorn University and a member of the Historical Commission at the Prime Minister's Office. In late 1996, Winai asked me, at that time based in Vientiane, to edit the journals for publication in Thailand. Having just finished a first draft in the summer of 1998, I received a letter from London. I considered it a lucky coincidence to learn that Turton was working on exactly the same material that I was editing. Without hesitation, I accepted Turton's kind offer to join the project, realising that the editing of the journals could benefit from a joint endeavour combining different research interests, approaches and disciplines.

A year later, back in Germany, our joint effort gained momentum. While I contextualised the diplomatic and political history to which the missions contributed, building on my familiarity with the indigenous histories of the Tai states and knowledge of their languages and scripts, Turton took the opportunity to conduct new research into the biography of the two envoys and the context of the new British colony in peninsular Burma and its relation with the government of British India in Calcutta. By the way, Turton's 'rediscovery' of the Maulmain Chronicle and other sources, kept in the Oriental and India Office Collections of the British Library, enabled him, the anthropologist-turned-historian, to write the first social and economic history of early colonial Moulmein and the Tennaserim provinces. Furthermore, we both traced and evaluated the various uses of the journals in the nineteenth and twentieth centuries. In the end, we had written two books in one: the annotated journals including various glossaries, and a history of Richardson and McLeod's pioneering 'travelling embassies' to Tai states. This is in short the rather intricate but most enjoyable journey towards our book *The Gold and Silver Road of Trade and Friendship* which – thus was our hope at least – might serve as a state-of-the-art-example of how to make archival material like the Richardson and McLeod diary journals accessible to a broad audience.

Deliberately chosen was the title of this first monograph-length study of an 'ethnography of embassy' that took place in an early-nineteenth century Tai context. 'The gold and silver road of trade and friendship', or some variant of this alluring phrase, epitomizes, in a way, the intents and aspirations of our two soldier-diplomats as well as the expectations of their Tai hosts. At Dr Richardson's first audience with a Tai ruler, mentioned at the start of this article, the *cao chiwit* ('Lord of Life', i.e. the King) of Lamphun said to his European guest that 'he was happy that the gold and silver road had been opened' (Farrington 2004: 27). There are several more local instances confirming that the Lan Na-Tenasserim borders were indeed considered 'golden, silver paths, free for traders' (Thongchai 1994: 73). The trade routes were also, in a very literal sense, gold and silver travelled, whether as currency or as tribute.[1] One central objective of the British missions of the 1830s, at least with regard to trade issues, was to secure the free cattle trade with Chiang Mai, Lamphun and other Tai Yuan principalities. Already during his first mission in early 1830, Richardson had become aware of serious disagreements among members of the Tai Yuan ruling elite. The ruler of Lamphun was receptive to British demands of free cattle trade with Moulmein and lower Burma but his relative in Chiang Mai, the energetic and powerful King Phutthawong (r. 1826–1846), was much more reluctant as he harboured deep suspicions against all things Burmese. Given the political tensions between Lamphun and Chiang Mai, Richardson was not even allowed to continue his journey to Chiang Mai. Instead, he had to wait until his second mission, four years later, to negotiate directly with Phutthawong and his ministers.

The British envoys did not always fully understand the political background of the internal conflicts in the Tai states they visited, nor were they aware of the need of their hosts to consult with their superiors in Bangkok, Ava or Pu'er. For example, when McLeod arrived in Chiang Rung, he was not allowed to continue his journey to Pu'er, the first major Chinese town beyond the borders of Sipsòng Panna. What had happened? Sipsòng Panna was one of the many smaller Tai states recognising the double suzerainty of two overlords, in her special case of China and Burma (conceptionalised as Sipsòng Panna's 'father' and 'mother' respectively). Unfortunately, one of the frequent dynastic feuds between a Chinese-backed and a Burmese-supported faction of the ruling house had flared up again. McLeod even learned some interesting details of that conflict from members of the 'pro-China' faction during his two-week long stay in Chiang Rung (Grabowsky & Turton 2003: 377). In return, his Tai Lü counterparts, especially the ruler (*cao fa*) of Chiang Lò, who was the chief minister in charge of foreign affairs, interrogated the British envoy on political events in Burma. It would be logical for the Chinese authorities in Pu'er to be suspicious of any foreigner with connections to Burma, and he was therefore reluctant to give McLeod permission to proceed on his journey. The Burmese suspected McLeod as well. During his ninth night in Chiang Rung, a Burman offical visited McLeod, informing him 'in confidence, that orders had been received from Kiang Túng on no account to permit me to proceed beyond the Mé Khong, and if I attempted to cross the river to take my head off; that the Burmans look upon me as a spy, and the Shans were partly inclined to do the same' (ibid. 382).

Tai records of the embassies

Given the historical context of the Richardson and McLeod missions as well as the circumstance that in several cases (like in Chiang Tung and Chiang Rung) they were even the first official encounters of a European power with these Tai states, one might expect that the missions were not only remembered but also recorded by the Tai themselves. We know from members of the French Mekong Exploration Commission who revisited many places in the Upper Mekong region thirty years after McLeod and Richardson that the 'white strangers' were vividly remembered by their former hosts even after such a long time. In August 1867, de Lagrée and another French officer met in Chiang Tung *cao fa* Maha Phom (1814/15-1876), who was a 22-year-old young man at the time of McLeod's visit. Maha Phom 'often spoke of the English officer, about his costume and his instrument, [as if] ... all these details had been to him the revelation of a superior civilization' (Garnier 1996, vol. 2: 65). Garnier does not tell the reader what kind of instrument the Chiang Tung ruler had exactly in mind. McLeod, however, recalls that he was asked by Maha Khanan 'to procure for him a four-barrel gun, a watch, compass, and twelve English sword blades, that would cut through a musket at a blow'! And he continues to wonder that Maha Khanan's eldest son 'wanted a double-barrel gun and watch for himself, a pair of pistols for his brother, and Puniah (Phaña) Wang a compass and thermometer'. De Carné, who himself was not present at the audience with Maha Khanan and his sons, was thinking more of dining utensils (knife, fork, spoon and wine glass) as the 'instruments' that had left a lasting impression on the people in Chiang Tung. Maha Phom also vividly remembered McLeod's awesome appetite: 'The king of Sien-Tong (Chiang Tung) remembered having seen a European officer, who passed his days in looking about him, and absorbing with a curious instrument [a fork?], three times more nourishment than a vigorous Laotian. This officer, with a robust appetite, was no other than Major M'Leod' (de Carné 1995: 195).

Do we find such remembrance also in indigenous records such as chronicles or other official writings? Let us start our investigation with the Chiang Tung Chronicle, the official annals of the Tai Khün state which records the political events until the establishment of British rule. Though the establishment of a British protectorate under J.G. Scott in 1890 is briefly recorded,[2] there is no entry on the McLeod's mission half a century earlier. However, we can find a short reference to it in the chronicle of one of Chiang Tung's dependencies. The Müang Yòng Chronicle has for the year *lai san* (AD 1836/37) the following entry: 'In that very year, a Kula came up to Chiang Tung as our state guest (*khaek müang*)'.[3] Kula, or its variant Kala, is a Tai (Yuan, Lü, Khün) generic term that designates western neighbours of the Yuan population of Lan Na like the Toung-su and the Shan.[4] Although British and other Europeans were generally called *kula khao* ('white stranger'), it seems highly probable that 'Kula' in the above quotation refers in fact to Captain McLeod.

On the last day of his sojourn in Chiang Rung, McLeod asked the chief minister for 'the history of the place', i.e. for a copy of the offical chronicle of Chiang Rung and Sipsòng Panna (Moeng Lü). Confronted with the foreigner's request, the minister 'looked serious', notes McLeod, commenting on the minister's reaction: '[A]fter considering a short time he asked me whether I wished he should lose his head; that there was but one copy, and that lodged in the palace, and though he afterwards promised to have extracts made for me from it, he never did so'. McLeod's entry of 25 March 1837 is the earliest confirmation of the existence of the Sipsòng Panna Chronicle, the oldest extant version of which was probably composed in 1864/65, not long after the death of Cao Suca Wanna (r. 1834–1864), who was the incumbent king (or *saenwi fa*) of Sipsòng Panna at the time of McLeod's visit.[5] There is little doubt that the European envoy's request embarrassed the minister, who might have considered the ruling dynasty's official history a kind of state secret, especially in such turbulent times of intra-dynastic conflicts. Neither the oldest extant version of the Sipsòng Panna Chronicle nor any later version mentions the appearance of a 'white stranger' in Chiang Rung in a single word. Though certainly a memorable event, at least in the eyes of all those Tai Lü nobles who personally encountered McLeod, the first European embassy to Chiang Rung was obviously not considered significant enough to be incorporated into the narrative of the country's official political history.

Whereas McLeod's travelling embassies to Chiang Tung and Chiang Rung were relatively brief, lasting only a period of about two weeks, Richardson's five missions to Lan Na (Chiang Mai, Lamphun and – on his third mission – also Lampang) added up to more than two years. Therefore, we might expect some mention in contemporary northern Thai sources. The Chiang Mai Chronicle, the most obvious choice for such a source, was composed probably in 1828 or perhaps a year later. Richardson's first mission of 1830 thus came a bit too late to be mentioned in the Chiang Mai Chronicle, whose narrative ends with the 'rebellion' of the Lao king Cao Anu in 1827. Half a century later, in 1875, just one year after the conclusion of the first Chiang Mai Treaty, King Chulalongkorn commissioned Phraya Maha Ammattayathibòdi to write a *Chronicle of Chiang Mai, Lampang, and Lamphun*. Starting with the Burmese invasion of Siam in 1767, the chronicle records the subsequent political history of western Lan Na until 1875/76 in the context of an anti-Burmese alliance between Bangkok and the Tai Yuan elite under the hegemony of the Siamese monarch. Neither the British missions of the 1830s nor those later missions of the 1860s and 1870s (Schomburgk, Edwardes) find a place in the chronicle's narrative. By the same token, Phraya Prachakitkòracak's influential Yonok Chronicle (1907), which heavily draws on the Chiang Mai Chronicle and Maha Ammattayathibòdi's work (1963 [1876]), among a number of other local sources, is completely silent on the McLeod and Richardson diplomatic missions.

However, there is one most interesting mention in a rare Tai Yuan manuscript of Dr Richardson's first visit to Lamphun in early 1830. The undated palm-leaf manuscript, the original of which is kept in Wat Phumin, Nan province, contains the following short statement: 'In CS 1191, a *kat pao* year (AD 1829/30) a Kula came to the town (*wiang*) of Lamphun'.[6] We do not know the author of the manuscript nor do we know its title.[7] The text has brief entries of memorable events for every year between 1728 (beginning of a successful anti-Burmese uprising in Lamphun) and 1854 (third Chiang Tung war). Most entries are not in particular concerned with 'big politics', and if so in a rather unorthodox manner. For example, we are informed that the Chiang Mai rulers maintained a kind of secret diplomacy with Burma, which might not have amused their Bangkok overlord: 'In CS 1243, a *ka mao* year [...], on the fourteenth day of the waning moon in the eighth month (27 May 1843), the Burmese king (*cao man*) arrived in Ciang Mai where he [and his retinue] stayed in five pavilions (*sala*)'. The bulk of the record, however, pertains to events that affected the people's daily life or were considered auspicious or unauspicious, such as foreign invasions, earthquakes, cholera epidemics and solar and lunar eclipses. Strongly resembling the Siamese Astrological Records (*cotmaihet hon*), the cumulative nature of the text points to several annalists primarily concerned with recording events for a kind of astrological calender. In this particular context, the first visit of a European to Lamphun in January 1830 was apparently of some significance for the annalist(s).

Richardson's 1839 mission in the eyes of Bangkok

The Tai Yuan principalities of northern Thailand were chief exporters of cattle to Moulmein. The procurement of cattle from these areas, linked with trade in horses and elephants for transport, was for the travelling embassies of Richardson and McLeod 'of equal if not greater importance than the possibility of trade with Yunnan', argues Turton in his discussion of cattle trade as a major theme of all British missions from Moulmein (Grabowsky & Turton 2003: 78). In the 1830s, epidemics like rinderpest and anthrax had dramatically reduced the cattle stock not only in Tenasserim, where it was insufficient to supply the growing demands of the British colony anyway, but also in Chiang Mai and other areas of the north. Disputes between the ruling elite of Chiang Mai, reluctant to allow any sale of cattle to British-Indian and Mon-Burmese traders, and the chiefs of Lamphun and Lampang, more flexible on this issue, had to be settled by their Siamese overlord. This was the main reason for Dr Richardson's final mission in 1839 which led him first to Bangkok via Nakhòn Chaisi. The Siamese government must have kept records of the diplomatic mission since the *Chronicle of the Third Reign*, written by Caophraya Thiphakòrawong in 1869/70 (Somjai 1983), containing a lengthy discussion of Richardson's audience with King Rama III, including a detailed list of gifts exchanged on that occasion; it also provides some background on the complicated negotiations between the British envoy and the Siamese authorities.[8] The Thai National Archives contain a contemporary source which might have been used by Caophraya Thiphakòrawong when writing his chapter on the British mission. It is an official, sealed letter (*san tra*) of Phraya Chakri to Chiang Mai 'concerning the prohibition to sell elephants, cows, and buffaloes to English traders (*phò kha*)'. The letter was issued 'on Sunday, the twelfth waning day of the fourth month, CS 1200, the year of the dog and first year of the decade (*cò samrittisok*)' or – if calculated in the Gregorian calendar – on Tuesday, 12 March 1839.[9] In a straightforward and unambiguous manner it takes the British request as serious as the arguments of the Chiang Mai ruler:

The Governor General of Bengal (*cao müang mangkala*) has sent a letter to the ministers (*senabòdi*) in Bangkok with the intention of promoting friendship (*camroen thang maitri*). He ordered Mr. Richardson to take [this letter] to Kanburi (Kanchanaburi). In this letter the Governor General of Bengal states that the English, Mon, and Indian (*khaek*) merchants, who came both by land and by sea to trade in the territory of Bangkok (i.e. Siam), relied on the mercy of His Majesty the King for buying and selling goods in a peaceful and normal way. The Governor General of Bangkok was aware of the power and benevolence of His Majesty the King and thus ordered Mr. Richardson to present this letter to His Majesty the King in a spirit of friendship. Mr. Richardson informed the high-ranking ministers that the English would like to sell goods in Chiang Mai, Lampang, and Lamphun. The English traders said that they asked [to buy] elephants, cows, and buffaloes from the local population who would sell elephants, cows, and buffaloes to the English traders. [But] the ruler of Chiang Mai forbade his subjects, who were the owners of the elephants, cows, and buffaloes, to sell them to the English traders. Mr. Richardson asked for the purchase of the elephants, cows, and buffaloes from the owners at the price [which had been agreed upon]. The response of the ministers to Mr. Richardson said that they were well aware that in the past English traders had come many times to Chiang Mai, Lampang, and Lamphun to make business and buy elephants, cows, and buffaloes from the local population. As to Mr. Richardson's allegation that Chiang Mai prohibited its citizens to sell elephants, cows, and buffaloes to English traders, the lord of that country (*cao khòng ban müang*) realised that elephants, cows, and buffaloes were dwindling in number. Since elephants, cows, and buffaloes were not normal goods, they should not be sold to outside the country. Elephants, cows, and buffaloes were of vital importance for the country. In times of war elephants and cows would transport provisions and therefore should be considered part of the military forces. Buffaloes were animals needed to do farming and thus secure the livelihood of the population.

Then Phraya Chakri affirms the King's commitment to maintain friendly relations (*ratcha maitri*) between Siam and England. These relations must not be put at stake by any high-handed attitudes towards the English envoy:

Thus a letter should be sent to Chiang Mai, Lampang, and Lamphun that a few (literally, 'two or three') elephants should be ar-

ranged for [Mr. Richardson] in a spirit of friendship. The ministers talked to Mr. Richardson in this way. Mr. Richardson agreed
with that proposal. [...] We have to maintain friendship [with Eng-
land] continuously. This friendship must not be destroyed. Phaya
Chiang Mai, Phaya Lakhòn, Phaya Lamphun and Phaya Uparat
[of Chiang Mai], Nai Phimasan, who are all relatives, and the officials (*saen thao*) have to talk with the Englishmen, thus the
friendly relations will not suffer. Elephants, cows, and buffaloes
have to be kept in sufficent numbers for the country (*ban-
müang*). The elephants, cows, and buffaloes must not decrease in
numbers, otherwise the country's future will be jeopardised.

In the end, the authorities of Chiang Mai, Lamphun and Lampang had
to pay compensation to the British traders for their financial losses
caused by the ban on the exports of cattle mentioned in Phraya Chakri's
letter. Richardson was not unsatisfied with the results of his negotiations with the Bangkok government. Putting all the blame on the vice-
roy (*cao hò na*) of Chiang Mai, 'being just now the obstacle and most
anxious to put a stop to the trade altogether', he remained cautiously
optimistic about the long-term prospects of the cattle trade, though he
did not overlook the 'jealousy' of the Siamese government concerning
'our influence' in the Siamese tributary states of western Lan Na (Farrington 2004: 222).

Conclusion

How should the Richardson and McLeod diplomatic missions be put
into a wider historical perspective? In how far were they mere agents of
British colonialism and imperialism in their manifold encounters with
local people of different social, ethnic and geographical backgrounds? It
is true that the official publication of the 1837 journals of Richardson
and McLeod as British Parliamentary Papers in 1869 was influenced by
the public debate in Britain about the feasibility of a railway route from
British India to southwestern China, but this debate already belongs to
a new stage of imperialist ambitions in the Far East. In the 1820s and
1830s, the geopolitical context was still very different (see Grabowsky &
Turton 2003: 3–21). The attitute of the two soldier diplomats towards
the 'indigenous peoples' and their cultures was likewise a far cry from
what the reports of late-nineteenth-century travelling diplomats exhibit.
Turton himself discussed this important aspect in his perceptive review
of G. H. Younghusband's (1888) *The Trans-Salwin State of Chiang Tung*
(2007), noting that there could be no sharper contrast between
McLeod's mission to Chiang Tung in 1837 and Younghusband's visit

half a century later. McLeod 'spoke excellent Burmese, and perhaps a little Tai. Younghusband knew almost nothing of the situation, spoke no relevant languages, and, moreover despised his interpreter, whereas McLeod's interpreter deputised for him and was of great assistance' (Turton 2007: 226). I fully agree with Turton's suggestion that we should think about the early modern 'ethographies of embassy' in a kind of post-colonial or even revisionist spirit, refraining from making 'anachronistic assumptions of imperialist teleology', and attributing agency and relative autonomy to both sides of a 'specific pre-imperialist encounter' (Turton 1998a: 21). Turton's passionate and somehow provocative plea for his approach to an 'ethnography of embassy' should be taken seriously.

Notes

1 Tribute missions from Tai tributary states, such as Babai (Lan Na) and Cheli (Sipsòng Panna) to Ming China almost regularly included gold and silver utensils of various kinds. See Liew-Herres & Grabowsky 2008: 31–33; and Grabowsky 2008: 56–59. As for the rhetorical use of the metaphoric phrase 'gold and silver road of trade and friendship', especially by Richardson, see Grabowsky & Turton 2003: xix.

2 'In the year [CS] 1252 the Gala Ingalik entered the state'. Quoted from Sao Saimöng 1981: 276.

3 *Tamnan Müang Yòng,* in Thawi 1984: 69–70 (in the original manuscript fᵒ 99)) [ดั่ง กูลาก็ขึ้นมาเป็นแขก เมืองเราเชียงตุงปีนั้นหั้นและ].

4 *Kula* (Transcription คุลา) is the Burmese word for foreigners (/kɔ`la/ kula;), notably natives of India. It is often written *kala* (Tr. คะลา). Later on, the word was misapplied to English and other Westerners who were sometimes called *kala/kula khao,* 'white strangers'.

5 The oldest extant version of the Moeng Lü Chronicle was discovered in 1940 by Li Fuyi, a Republican official in Chiang Rung (Jinghong) who translated it into Chinese a few years later. During the final phase of the war, however, the original manuscript got lost. For details, see Liew-Herres et al. forthcoming.

6 Saraswadee 1991: 28 (fᵒ 34/3) [สักกะ 1191 ตัว ปีกัด เป้าแล คุลามาเวียงลพูนแล, *sakka 1191 tua pi kat pao lae kula ma wiang lapun lae*].

7 The title *Cotmaihet lan na* (Records of Lan Na) is an artificial one given by the staff of the Social Research Institute, Chiang Mai University, where a microfilm-copy is kept under the code number SRI 82.107.05.048-048.

8 Thiphakòrawong 1961: 196–99. *The Chronicle of the State Reception of European Ambassadors in the Early Bangkok Period,* first published in 1936, has reproduced Thiphakòrawong's record of the 1839 Richardson mission almost verbatim. See Thailand 1969: 286–292.

9 The document (สารตราเจ้าพระยาจักรีถึงเมืองเชียงใหม่ เรื่องห้ามขายช้าง โค กระบือให้พ่อค้าอังกฤษ จ.ศ. ๑๒๐๐, *santra cao phraya cakkri thüng müang chiang mai rüang ham khai chang kho krabü hai phò kha angrit c.s. 1200*) is published in Winai 1999: 33–44.

Kengtung: sawbwa's *haw* or palace, c. 1890

Source: British Library, Oriental and India Office Collections (Sir J. George Scott collection)

Appendix

Andrew Turton – A Select Bibliography

Books

2008 *khitcamkat khongkankhrobngam thang udomkan.* [transl. Utong Prasasvinitchai] Bangkok: Namrin.

2003 With Volker Grabowsky *The gold and silver road of trade and friendship: the McLeod and Richardson diplomatic missions to Tai states in 1837.* Chiang Mai, Silkworm Books, pp. 624.

2000 Edited *Civility and savagery: social identities in Tai states.* London, Curzon, pp. 376.

1991 Edited (with Manas Chitakasem) *Thai constructions of knowledge.* London, SOAS, pp. 212. [reprinted 1995]

1989 Edited (with Gill Hart & Ben White) *Agrarian transformations: local processes and the state in Southeast Asia.* Berkeley, University of California Press, pp. 341. [first paperback printing 1992]

1988 Edited (with John G. Taylor) *Sociology of 'developing societies': Southeast Asia.* New York, Monthly Review Press, London, Macmillan, pp. 279.

1987 *Production, power and participation in rural Thailand: experiences of poor farmers' groups.* Geneva, UNRISD, pp. 134.

1984 Edited (with Shigeharu Tanabe) *History and peasant consciousness in South East Asia.* Senri Ethnological Studies No. 13, National Museum of Ethnology, Osaka, pp. 420.

1978 Edited (with Jonathan Fast & Malcolm Caldwell) *Thailand: roots of conflict.* Nottingham, Spokesman, pp. 196.

1976 *Northern Thai peasant society: a case study of jural and political structures at the village level and their twentieth century transformations.* University of London Microfilms. PhD thesis, University of London, pp. 672.

1974 Edited *Peoples of the Earth Volume 11, South East Asia,* New York, Danbury Press, pp. 144.

Pamphlets

1979 Edited Malcolm Caldwell 1931-78 a tribute and a bibliography. Nottingham, Spokesman, p. 80.
   – Malcolm Caldwell as teacher and writer. Ibid. pp. 17-23.
   – Bibliography of the writings of Malcolm Caldwell. Ibid. pp. 71-80.
1978 (with others) *Political repression in Thailand*. London, ECCSTP, p. 66.

Contributions to books

2008 Disappointing gifts. In Nikolai Ssorin-Chaikov (ed.) *Diplomatic gifts*. Routledge.
2004 Violent Capture of People for Exchange on Karen-Tai Borders in the 1830s. In Gwyn Campbell (ed.), *The Structure of Slavery in Indian Ocean, Africa and Asia*. London, Frank Cass.
2001 Delay and deception in Tai-British diplomatic encounters of the early 19th century. In Joy Hendry and C.W. Watson (eds.) *An anthropology of indirect communication*. ASA Monographs 37. London, Routledge. pp. 271-89.
2000 Inter-ethnic relations in Tai political domains. In Andrew Turton (ed.) *Civility and savagery: social identity in Tai states*. London, Curzon, pp. 1-32.
   – Internal histories and comparisons: introduction. Ibid. pp. 33-37.
   – Thai-Malay borderlands: introduction. Ibid. pp. 159-61.
   – Laos: a poly-ethnic state: introduction. Ibid. pp. 201-5.
   – Lanna and neighbours: introduction. Ibid. pp. 291-3.
1998 Thai institutions of slavery [revised and expanded]. In Georges Condominas (ed.) *Formes extrêmes de dépendance: contributions à l'étude de l'esclavage en Asie du Sud-Est*. Paris, Editions de L'Ecole des Hautes Etudes en Sciences Sociales, pp. 411-57.
1991 State poetics and civil rhetoric. In Manas Chitakasem and Andrew Turton (eds.) *Thai constructions of knowledge*. London, SOAS, pp. 1-14.
   – Invulnerability and local knowledge. Ibid. pp.155-82.
1990 Thailand. In Robert H.Taylor (ed.) *Asia and the Pacific, Handbooks to the Modern World series*. Facts on File, New York and Oxford, pp. 836-51.
   Reflections on 'cultural approaches' to development. In Abdul Aziz Saleh and D.Flud van Giffen (eds.) *Socio-cultural impacts of development: some theoretical issues*. Padang, Andalas University

Research Center, pp. 63-75.
banda amnat thongthin kap kan yaektua tang sangkhom nai chonnabot. In Ananya Bhuchongkul (ed.) *rat kap muuban nai thai suksa* [State and village in Thai studies]. Bangkok, Thai Khadi Research Institute, pp. 31-74. [transl. of 1989 'Local powers ...']

1989 Thailand: agrarian bases of state power. In G. Hart, A. Turton & B. White (eds.) *Agrarian transformations: local processes and the state in Southeast Asia.* Berkeley, University of California Press, pp. 53-69.
– Local powers and rural differentiation. Ibid. pp. 70-97.
– Introduction (with Gillian Hart & Benjamin White). Ibid. pp. I-II.

1988 Ideological commodity production. In John G. Taylor & Andrew Turton (eds.) *Sociology of 'developing societies': Southeast Asia.* New York, Monthly Review Press, London, Macmillan, pp. 207-10.
– Introduction (with John G. Taylor). Ibid. 1-13.
– Rural transformations and agrarian differentiation. Ibid. pp. 107-9.
– Culture and ideology. Ibid. pp. 177-9.
– Ethnic histories and minority identities. Ibid. pp. 211-13.

1987 Thailand. In Gillian Moore (ed.) *The ASEAN countries.* Library of Nations series, London, Time Life Books, pp. 128-45.

1986 Patrolling the middle-ground: methodological perspectives on 'everyday peasant resistance'. In James C. Scott and Benedict J. Tria Kerkvliet (eds.) *Everyday forms of peasant resistance in South East Asia.* Library of Peasant Studies No. 9, London, Frank Cass, pp. 36-48.

1984 Limits of ideological domination and the formation of social consciousness. In Andrew Turton & Shigeharu Tanabe (eds.) *History and peasant consciousness in South East Asia.* Senri Ethnological Studies No. 13, Osaka: National Museum of Ethnology, pp. 19-73.
– Introduction (with Shigeharu Tanabe). Ibid. pp. 1-18.

1982 Poverty, reform and class struggle in rural Thailand. In Steve Jones, P.C. Joshi & Miguel Murmis (eds.) *Rural poverty and agrarian reform.* Enda, Dakar, and Allied Publishers, New Delhi, pp. 20-45.

1980 Thai institutions of slavery. In James L.Watson (ed.) *Asian and African systems of slavery.* Oxford, Blackwell, pp. 251-92.

1978 Architectural and political space in Thailand. In G. Milner (ed.) *Natural symbols in South East Asia,* London, SOAS, pp. 113-32.
satanakan patuban nai chonnabot thai. In fai wichakan (eds.) *sethakhit thai: khrongsang kap kan plianplaeng: ruam botkwam dan sethasat kanmuang* [Structure and change in the Thai economy: collected papers in political economy]. Bangkok, Khanasethasat,

Mahawithayalai chulalongkorn, pp. 45-72. [translation of 1978 'The current situation ...'] reprinted 1979, 1982.
Exploitation of the Thai peasantry. In Kamla Bhasin & R. Vimala (eds.) *Readings in poverty, politics and development*. New Delhi, FAO Freedom from Hunger Campaign: Action for Development, pp. 107-11. [summary of 1978 'The current situation ...']
The current situation in the Thai countryside. In Andrew Turton, Jonathan Fast & Malcolm Caldwell (eds.) *Thailand: roots of conflict*. Nottingham, Spokesman, pp. 104-42.
Preface. Ibid. pp. 1-2.
Interview with the President of the Northern Region, Peasants Federation of Thailand. September 1976. Ibid. pp. 183-7.

Articles

2006   Remembering local history: Kuba Wajiraphanya (c1853-1928), Phra Thongthip and the Müang way of life. *Journal of the Siam Society*. Vol. 94, pp. 147-76.
1999   Diplomatic missions to Tai states by David Richardson and W.C. McLeod 1830-1839. *Journal of the Siam Society*, Vol. 86, Nos. 1 and 2, pp. 9-25.
1997   Ethnography of embassy: anthropological readings of records of diplomatic encounters between Britain and Tai states in the early nineteenth century. *South East Asia Research*, 5 (2), pp. 175-205.
1987   'Invulnerability', local knowledge and popular resistance: a Thai theme in
South East Asian perspective. *Proceedings of the 3rd International Conference on Thai Studies*. Canberra, Australian National University, pp. 363-74.
1986   Patrolling the middle-ground: methodological perspectives on 'everyday peasant resistance'. *Journal of Peasant Studies*. 13 (2), pp. 36-48.
1984   People of the same spirit: local matrikin groups and their cults. *Mankind*. 14 (3), pp. 272-85.
1982   Utilisation et signification des structures physiques de l'architecture domestique dans une population de Thailande du Nord. *Les Cahiers de L'A.D.R.I.* (Paris), 6/7, pp. 63-103.
       Participating in rural development: some aspects of the Thai case. *Akademika* (Journal of Humanities and Social Sciences, Universiti Kebangsaan Malaysia). 20 & 21, pp. 115-47.
1980   The Thai house: domestication of ideology. *Architectural Association Quarterly*. 12 (2), pp. 4-11.

1977 Laos: a peasant people's struggle for national liberation. *Race and class.* 18 (3), pp. 279-92.

1976 Northern Thai peasant society: twentieth century transformations in political and jural structures. *Journal of Peasant Studies.* 18 (3), pp. 267-98.
Tai. In *Family of Man* 7.88, London, Marshall Cavendish, pp. 2437-9.
Thai. In *Family of Man* 7.89, London, Marshall Cavendish, pp. 2475-7.

1974 National minority peoples of Indochina. *Journal of Contemporary Asia.* 4 (3), pp. 336-43. [Author's name was omitted due to editorial oversight.]

1972 Matrilineal descent groups and spirit cults of the Thai-yuan in northern Thailand. *Journal of the Siam Society.* 60 (2), pp. 217-56.
Blank coup in Thailand. *New Left Review.* 71, pp. 36-43. [pseud. Daniel Lee]

Other materials

The above bibliography omits various classes of material, including:
– work in progress and planned;
– selected unpublished papers, such as:

1993 Localisation and domestication: approaches to Khon Müang concepts of 'environment'. Nordic Institute for Asian Studies, Copenhagen.

1980 Rituals of expulsion. Centre for South East Asian Studies, SOAS.

1974 'Less absurd nonsense?' Anthropology and the knowledge of ideology: some elements of a theory of superstructure. London Intercollegiate Anthropology Seminar.

– anonymous publications in *Indochina* (Journal of the Indochina Solidarity Conference) 1971, 1973, 1975; and *Vietnam International* (ed. Peggy Duff, International Confederation for Peace and Disarmament) 1972, 1976.
– non-academic publications in magazines, newspapers etc. mainly since 1959;
– book reviews;
– translations and reprints of articles in books, anthologies, readers and textbooks;
– forewords to books;
– academic policy reports, from 1988.

Notes on Contributors

Anan Ganjanapan is a Professor of Anthropology in the Department of Sociology and Anthropology at Chiangmai University. With a Ph.D. from Cornell, he has published *Local Control of Land and Forest: Cultural Dimension of Resource Management in Northern Thailand* (RCSD, 2000) besides influential articles such as 'Globalization and the process of Culture in Thailand' in *Globalization in Southeast Asia* (ed. Shinji Yamashita & J.S. Eades, Berghahn 2003) and others on community forestry and participatory watershed development.

Paul T. Cohen is Associate Professor and Senior Research Fellow in the Department of Anthropology at Macquarie University where he has taught since 1970. He has specialized on the Tai Lue of Northern Thailand and the Akha of Muang Singh in Laos, and on issues of agrarian change and ethnicity. Besides a wide range of major articles on Buddhist pilgrimage and local-level politics, land reform and irrigation associations, border trade and opium trafficking in the Thai-Mekong region, he has co-edited *Health and Development in Southeast Asia* (ANU 1995) and *The Political Economy of Primary Health Care in Southeast Asia* (ADS/ASEAN 1989).

Jim Glassman is Associate Professor in the Department of Geography at the University of British Columbia (Vancouver, Canada). His research focuses on the political economy of development in Southeast Asia, with special emphasis on industrialisation, state power and social struggles over development. His most recently completed work has been conducted in Thailand and elsewhere in the Greater Mekong Subregion, including Yunnan province of China. He is currently conducting research on the role of Cold War geopolitics in shaping regional business networks in East and Southeast Asia. He is the author of *Thailand at the Margins* (Oxford University Press, 2004).

Volker Grabowsky is Professor of Thai Studies at the Asia-Africa-Institute, University of Hamburg. He has specialized in the history and culture of the Tai peoples in northern Thailand and Laos. Among his more recent publications are *The Gold and Silver Road of Trade and*

Friendship: The McLeod and Richardson Diplomatic Missions to Tai States in 1837 (with Andrew Turton, Chiang Mai 2003) and *Chronicles of Chiang Khaeng: A Tai Lü Principality of the Upper Mekong* (with Renoo Wichasin, Honolulu 2008).

Philip Hirsch received his doctorate in social anthropology from the School of Oriental and African Studies, University of London, in 1987, for a thesis carried out under the supervision of Andrew Turton. He is Professor of Human Geography in the School of Geosciences at the University of Sydney. He directs the Australian Mekong Resource Centre and has research interests in river basin management, environmental and social impacts of development, agrarian transitions and the politics of land, natural resources and the environment. He is involved in an agrarian transitions programme that includes restudies of villages studied during PhD fieldwork. Publications include *Development Dilemmas in Rural Thailand* (Oxford University Press 1990), *The Politics of Environment in Southeast Asia: resources and resistance* (ed. with Carol Warren, Routledge 1998) and other publications on environmental and development issues in Southeast Asia.

Jamaree Chiengthong is Associate Professor and former Head of the Department of Sociology and Anthropology at Chiangmai University, Thailand. Her doctorate in social anthropology was supervised by Andrew Turton. She has published widely on rural development and gender and regional issues, specializing in rural transformations in northern Thailand and Laos. Her publications include 'The politics of ethnicity, indigenous culture and knowledge in Thailand' in *Social Challenges for the Mekong Region* (ed. Mingsarn Kaosa-ard and John Dore, SRI, Chiangmai 2003) and (in Thai) 'Studies in Thai Society and Thai relations' in *The State of Thai Studies: A Critical Survey* (ed. Chatthip Nartsupha, Silkworm, Chiangmai 2000) and *The Evolution of Thai Civil Society* (Thailand Development and Research Institute, Bangkok 2000).

Charles Keyes is Professor Emeritus of Anthropology and International Studies at the University of Washington and former President of the Association for Asian Studies. He has carried out extensive research in Thailand, Vietnam, Laos and Cambodia. He has authored, edited or co-edited 14 books, monographs or special issues of journals and published over 80 articles. His major publications include *On the Margins of Asia: Diversity in Asian States* (ed. AAS 2006); *Cultural Crisis and Social Memory: Modernity and Identity in Thailand and Laos* (edited with Shigeharu Tanabe, RoutledgeCurzon 2002); *The Golden Peninsula: Culture and Adaptation in Mainland Southeast Asia* (reprinted, University of Hawaii Press 1995); *Thailand: Buddhist Kingdom as Modern Nation State*

(Westview, 1987) and *Asian Visions of Authority: Religion and the Modern States of East and Southeast Asia* (edited with Laurel Kendall and Helen Hardacre, University of Hawaii Press 1994).

Craig J. Reynolds is Adjunct Professor in the College of Asia and the Pacific, Australian National University. He has published widely on the social, cultural and intellectual history of Thailand and Southeast Asia. His most recent book is *Seditious Histories: Contesting Thai and Southeast Asian Pasts* (University of Washington Press 2006). 'The Professional Lives of O. W. Wolters' in his edited *O. W. Wolters, Early Southeast Asia: Selected Essays*, was published in 2008 by Cornell University's Southeast Asia Programme. His current research project concerns religion, policing, banditry and the environment in Thailand's midsouth, 1920s-1960s.

Jonathan Rigg is a Professor of Geography at Durham University. His research interests are in agrarian change and rural-urban relations in Southeast Asia, with a focus on Thailand and Laos. He is the author of *Southeast Asia: the human landscape of modernisation and development* (Routledge, 2003), *Living with transition in Laos: market integration in Southeast Asia* (Routledge: 2005) and is the editor of a three-volume reader, *Southeast Asian development: critical concepts in the social sciences* (Routledge, 2008).

Nicholas Tapp is a Professor in the Department of Anthropology at the Australian National University, whose doctorate was also supervised by Andrew Turton. His research has focused on the society and culture of the Hmong people and he has conducted extensive fieldwork in Thailand and China besides shorter periods of fieldwork in France, Canada, the USA, Australia, Laos and Vietnam. He has published a number of articles on subjects ranging from diaspora to political participation and directs the Thai-Yunnan Project at the ANU. His books include *Sovereignty and Rebellion: the White Hmong of Northern Thailand* (Oxford University Press, 1989) and *The Hmong of China: Agency, Context, and the Imaginary* (Brill 201) besides other edited or co-edited publications and papers.

References

Adamson, Walter L. 2002 'Gramsci and the Politics of Civil Society', in James Martin (ed.) *Antonio Gramsci: Critical Assessments of Leading Practical Philosophers* (vol. 2: Marxism, Philosophy and Politics). London and New York: Routledge.

Agamben, Giorgio 1998 *Homo Sacer: Sovereign Power and Bare Life*. Palo Alto: Stanford University Press.

– 2005 *State of Exception*. Chicago: University of Chicago Press.

Agarwal, Bina 2001 'Participatory exclusions, community forestry, and gender: an analysis for South Asia and a conceptual framework', *World Development* 29 (10). 1623-1648.

Akin Rabibhadana 1969 *The Social Organization of Thai Society in the Early Bangkok Period, 1782-1873*. (Data Paper no. 74). Ithaca: Department of Asian Studies, Cornell University.

Allen, D. 1989 'Antiwar Asian Scholars and the Vietnam/Indochina War', *Bulletin of Concerned Asian Scholars* 21 (2-4). 112-134.

Althusser, Louis (1968) 1971 'Ideology and Ideological State Apparatuses: Notes towards an Investigation', in his *Lenin and Philosophy and Other Essays*. London: Monthly Review Press (New Left Books).

Anan Ganjanapan 1984 'The Idiom of *Phi Ka*: Peasant Conception of Class Differentiation in Northern Thailand', *Mankind* 14 (4) (Special issue on Spirit Cults and the Position of Women in Northern Thailand, ed. Paul Cohen & Gehan Wijeyewardene). 325-329.

– 1989 'Conflicts over the deployment and control of labor in a northern Thai village', in Gillian Hart, Andrew Turton & Benjamin White (ed.) *Agrarian Transformations: Local Processes and the State in Southeast Asia*. Berkeley: University of California Press. 98-122.

– 1997 'The politics of environment in northern Thailand: ethnicity and highland development programmes', in Philip Hirsch (ed.) *Seeing Forests for Trees: Environmentalism in Thailand*. Chiang Mai: Silkworm Books. 202-222.

– 2003 'Complexity of rights and legal pluralism in participatory watershed development in Thailand', in Xu Jianchu & Stephen Mikesell (ed.) *Landscapes of Diversity: Indigenous Knowledge, Sustainable Livelihoods and Resources Governance in Montane Mainland Southeast Asia*. Kunming: Yunnan Science and Technology Press. 207-12.

Anderson, Benedict 1977 'Withdrawal Symptoms: Social and Cultural Aspects of the October 6 Coup', *Bulletin of Concerned Asian Scholars*. 9 (3). 13-30.

– 1978 'Studies of the Thai State: the State of Thai Studies', in Eliezer B. Ayal (ed.) *The Study of Thailand: Analyses of Knowledge, Approaches, and Prospects in Anthropology, Art History, Economics, History, and Political Science*. Athens, Ohio: Ohio Center for International Studies. 193-247.

– 1990 'Murder and Progress in Modern Siam', *New Left Review*. 181. 33-48.

– 1998 *The Spectre of Comparisons: Nationalism, Southeast Asia and the World*. London and New York: Verso.

Archer, Margaret 2000 *Being Human: The Problem of Agency*. Cambridge: Cambridge University Press.

Arghiros, Daniel 1993 Rural Transformation and Local Politics in a Central Thai District. Unpub. Ph.D thesis, University of Hull.

– 2001 *Democracy, Development and Decentralization in Provincial Thailand.* Richmond: Curzon Press.

Baker, Chris & Pasuk Phongpaichit 2005 *A History of Thailand.* Cambridge: Cambridge University Press.

Bell, Catherine 1989 'Religion and Chinese Culture: Towards an Assessment of Popular Religion', *History of Religions* 29 (1). 35-57.

– 1992 *Ritual Theory, Ritual Practice.* New York and London: Routledge.

Bell, Peter 1978 'Cycles of Class Struggle in Thailand', *Journal of Contemporary Asia* 8 (1). 51-79.

– 1982 'Western Conceptions of Thai Society: The Politics of American Scholarship', *Journal of Contemporary Asia* 12 (1). 61-74.

– 2003 'Thailand's Economic Crisis: A New Cycle of Social Struggle,' in G.J. Ungpakorn (ed). *Radicalising Thailand: New Political Perspectives.* Bangkok: Institute of Asian Studies, Chulalongkorn University. 41-74.

Benjamin, Walter (1940) 1969 'Theses on the Philosophy of History', in his *Illuminations: Essays and Reflections.* New York: Schocken.

– (1921) 1977 'Critique of Violence', in *Walter Benjamin: Selected Writings, 1913-26* (Vol. I). London: Verso.

Berman, Marshall 1990 *All That is Solid Melts into Air.* London: Verso.

Bloch, Maurice (ed.) 1975 *Political Language and Oratory in Traditional Society.* London and New York: The Academic Press.

– 1977 'The Past and the Present in the Present', *Man* (New Series). 12 (2). 278-92.

– 1982 *Prey into Hunter: the Politics of Religious Experience.* Cambridge: Cambridge University Press.

– 1985 'From Cognition to Ideology', in Richard Fardon (ed.) *Power and Knowledge: anthropological and sociological approaches.* Edinburgh: Scottish Academic Press.

– 1986 *From Blessing to Violence: history and ideology in the circumcision ritual of the Merina of Madagascar.* Cambridge: Cambridge University Press.

– 1991 'Language, Anthropology and Cognitive Science', *Man* (New Series). 26 (2). 183-98.

Bloch, Maurice & Jonathan Parry 1991 'Introduction: Money and The Morality of Exchange' in their (ed.) *Money and the Morality of Exchange.* Cambridge: Cambridge University Press.

Bourdieu, Pierre 1977 *Outline of a Theory of Practice.* Cambridge and New York: Cambridge University Press.

– (1963) 1979 'The Kabyle House, or, the world reversed', in his *Algeria 1960: Essays.* Cambridge and New York: Cambridge University Press.

– 1990 *The Logic of Practice.* Cambridge: Polity Press.

Bowie, Katherine 1988 Peasant Perspectives on the Political Economy of the Northern Thai Kingdom of Chiangmai in the Nineteenth Century. Unpublished Ph.D thesis, University of Illinois.

– 1996 'Slavery in Nineteenth-Century Northern Thailand: Archival Anecdotes and Villages Voices' in E. Paul Durrenburger (ed.) *State Power and Culture in Thailand.* (Monograph No. 44). New Haven: Yale Southeast Asian Studies Programme, Yale University. 100-38.

– 1997 *Rituals of National Loyalty: An Anthropology of the State and The Village Scout Movement in Thailand.* New York: Columbia University Press.

Brailey, Nigel J. 1968 The Origins of the Siamese Forward Movement in Western Laos, 1855-1892. Unpub. Ph.D. thesis, School of Oriental and African Studies, University of London.

Brummelhuis, Han ten 2005 *King of the Waters: Homan van der Heide and the Origin of Modern Irrigation in Siam.* Leiden: KITLV Press.

Brun, Viggo 1990 'Traditional Manuals and the Transmission of Knowledge in Thailand', in Birthe Arendup et. al. (ed.) *The Master Said: to Study and ...; to Soren Egerod on the Occasion of His Sixty-Seventh Birthday* (Occ. Paps. 6). Copenhagen: University of Copenhagen.

Brun, Viggo & Trond Schumacher 1987 *Traditional Herbal Medicine in Northern Thailand*. Berkeley: University of California Press.

Butler, Judith, Ernesto Laclau & Slavoj Žižek 2000 *Contingency, Hegemony, Universality: Contemporary dialogues on the Left*. London and New York: Verso.

Chatchai Panananon 1982 'Siamese "Slavery": The Institution and its Abolition'. Unpub. PhD thesis, University of Michigan.

Chatthip Nartsupha 1984 'The Ideology of "Holy Men" Revolts in North East Thailand', in Andrew Turton & Shigeharu Tanabe (ed.) *History and Peasant Consciousness in South East Asia*. (Senri Ethnological Studies No. 13). Osaka: National Museum of Ethnology. 111-134.

— 1991 'The Community Culture School of Thought', in Manas Chitakasem & Andrew Turton (ed.) *Thai Constructions of Knowledge*. London: School of Oriental and African Studies, University of London.

Chhotray, Vasudha 2004 'The negation of politics in participatory development projects, Kurnool, Andhra Pradesh', *Development and Change* 35(2). 327-352.

Chomsky, Noam 1988 *The Culture of Terrorism*. Boston: South End Press.

Cohen, Abner 1976 *Two-dimensional man: an essay on the anthropology of power and symbolism in complex society*. Berkeley: University of California Press.

— 1993 *Masquerade politics: explorations in the study of urban cultural movements*. Berkeley: University of California Press.

Cohen, Anjalee P. 2006 Youth Culture and Identity: Consumerism, Drugs and Gangs in Chiang Mai, Northern Thailand. Unpub. PhD thesis, Macquarie University.

Cohen, Paul T. 1987 'From Moral Regeneration to Confrontation: Two Paths to Equality in the Political Rhetoric of a Northern Thai Peasant Leader', *Mankind* 17(2) (Special Issue No. 5, on Equality and Inequality: Papers in Memory of Chandra Jayawardena, ed. Ian Bedford, Gillian Bottomley & Annette Hamilton). 153-167.

— 2001 'Buddhism Unshackled: The Yuan "Holy Man" Tradition and the Nation-State in the Tai World', *Journal of Southeast Asian Studies* 32(2). 227-247.

Condominas, Georges, et al. 1998 *Formes extrêmes de dependence. Contributions á l'étude de l'esclavage en Asie du Sud-Est*. (Civilisations et sociétés, 96). Paris: École des Hautes Études en Sciences Sociales.

Connerton, Paul 1989 *How Societies Remember*. Cambridge and New York: Cambridge University Press.

Connors, M.K. 2007 *Democracy and National Identity in Thailand*. Copenhagen: Nordic Institute of Asian Studies Press.

— 2008 'Article of Faith: The Failure of Royal Liberalism in Thailand', *Journal of Contemporary Asia* 38 (1). 143-167.

Connors, M.K. & Hewison, K. 2008 'Introduction: Thailand and the "Good Coup"', *Journal of Contemporary Asia* 38 (1). 1-10.

Cornwall, Andrea 2003 'Whose voices? Whose choices? Reflections on gender and participatory development', *World Development* 31(8). 1325-1342.

Cruikshank, R. B. 1975 'Slavery in Nineteenth Century Siam', *Journal of the Siam Society* 63.2 (July). 315-333.

Cumings, B. 1990 *The Origins of the Korean War, Volume II: The Roaring of the Cataract, 1947-1950*. Princeton: Princeton University Press.

Dārārat Mēttārikānon. 2003. *Kānmüang song fang khōng: Ngān khonkwā wicai radap prinyā ēk không Culālongkôn Mahāwithayālai rüang kānruam klum thāng kānmüang khong sô. sô. Īsān Phô. Sô, 2476-2494* (Politics on the two sides of the Mekhong: Ph.D. Dissertation at Chulalongkorn University concerning unity of members of parliament, 1933-1951). Bangkok: Matichon.

Davis, David Brion 1966 *The Problem of Slavery in Western Culture*. Ithaca: Cornell University Press.

de Carné, Louis (1872) 1995 *Travels in Indo-China and the Chinese Empire* (translation from the French). London: Chapman and Hall [reprinted 1995, as *Travels on the Mekong: Cambodia, Laos and Yunnan*. Bangkok: White Lotus].

Deleuze, Gilles & Felix Guattari 1983 *Anti-Oedipus: Capitalism and Schizophrenia*. Minneapolis: University of Minnesota Press.

Derrida, Jacques 2002 'The Force of Law: "the mystical foundation of authority"', in his *Acts of Religion*. London and New York: Routledge.

Dixon, Chris 1999 *The Thai economy: uneven development and internationalization*. London: Routledge.

Doignon, Jean-Paul & Jean-Claude Falmagne 1985 'Spaces for the assessment of knowledge', *International Journal of Man-Machine Studies* 23. 175-196.

Duncan, Christopher R. (ed.) 2004 *Civilizing the Margins: Southeast Asian Government Policies for the Development of Minorities*. Ithaca, NY: Cornell University Press.

Edwardes 1875 'Report by Mr. Edwardes Respecting Chiengmai and other Teak Districts of Siam', in *Commercial Reports by Her Majesty's Consular Officers in Siam for the Year 1874*. London: Harrison and Sons, 10–23 [British Library, India Office & Oriental Collections].

Evans, Grant (ed.) 1993 *Asia's Cultural Mosaic: An Anthropological Introduction*. New York and London: Prentice Hall.

Farrington, Anthony (ed.) 2004 *Dr Richardson's Missions to Siam 1829-1839*. Bangkok: White Lotus.

Feeny, David 1989 'The Decline of Property Rights in Man in Thailand, 1800-1913', *Journal of Economic History* 49 (2). 285-296.

– 1993 'The Demise of Corvée and Slavery in Thailand, 1782-1913', in Klein, Martin A. (ed.) *Breaking the Chains: Slavery, Bondage, and Emancipation in Modern Africa and Asia*. Madison: University of Wisconsin Press.

Fentress, James & Chris Wickham 1992 *Social Memory*. Oxford and Cambridge, Mass: Basil Blackwell.

Ferguson, James 1990 *The anti-politics machine: 'development', depoliticization, and bureaucratic power in Lesotho*. Cambridge: Cambridge University Press.

Feuchtwang, Stephan 1975 'Chinese Religion', in Maurice Bloch (ed.) *Marxist Analyses and Social Anthropology*. London: Malaby Press.

Filmer, Paul 2003 'Structures of feeling and socio-cultural formations: the significance of literature and experience to Raymond Williams' sociology of culture', *British Journal of Sociology* 54 (2). 199-219.

Firth, Raymond 1964 *Essays on Social Organization and Values*. London: The Athlone Press.

Fiskesjö, Magnus 2003 *The Thanksgiving Turkey Pardon, the Death of Teddy's Bear, and the Sovereign Exception of Guantanamo*. Chicago: Prickly Paradigm Press.

Flood, Thadeus 1977 *The United States and the Military Coup in Thailand: A Background Study*. Berkeley: Indochina Resource Center.

Fogel, Robert & Stanley Engerman 1974 *Time on the Cross*. Boston: Little Brown.

Foucault, Michel 1977 *Language, Counter-memory, Practice: Selected Interviews and Notes* (Ed. D.F. Bouchard). Ithaca: Cornell University Press.

Friedmann, John 1992 *Empowerment: the politics of alternative development*. Oxford: Basil Blackwell.

Garfinkel, Harold 1967 *Studies in Ethnomethodology*. Englewood Cliffs, NJ: Prentice-Hall.

Garnier, Francis 1996 *Further Travels in Laos and in Yunnan* Vol. 2 (transl. by Walter E.J. Tips). Bangkok: White Lotus.

Gawin Chutima 1990 *The Rise and Fall of the Communist Party of Thailand (1973-1987)*. Canterbury: Centre of South-East Asian Studies.

Geertz, Clifford 1983a 'Common Sense as a Cultural System', in his *Local Knowledge: Further Essays in Interpretive Anthropology*. New York: Basic Books.

– 1983b '"From the Native's Point of View": On the Nature of Anthropological Understanding', in his *Local Knowledge: Further Essays in Interpretive Anthropology*. New York: Basic Books.

Genovese, Eugene 1969 *The World the Slaveholders Made: Two Essays in Interpretation*. New York: Pantheon Books.

Glassman, Jim 2002 'From Seattle (and Ubon) to Bangkok: the Scales of Resistance to Corporate Globalization,' *Environment and Planning D: Society and Space* 20 (5). 513-533.

– 2004a *Thailand at the Margins: Internationalization of the State and the Transformation of Labour*. Oxford and New York: Oxford University Press.

– 2004b 'Economic "Nationalism" in a Post-Nationalist Era: The Political Economy of Economic Policy in Post-crisis Thailand', *Critical Asian Studies* 36 (1). 37-64.

– 2005 'The "War on Terrorism" comes to Southeast Asia', *Journal of Contemporary Asia* 35 (1). 3-28.

– 2009 'The Decline of the Left and Political Devolution in Thailand', *Human Geography* 2, 1.

– (forthcoming) 'Thailand in the Era of the Cold War and Rama IX', in Mark Pavlick (ed). *US War Crimes in Indochina: An Unfinished Agenda*. Monroe: Common Courage Press.

Goffman, Erving 1959 *The Presentation of Self in Everyday Life*. New York: Anchor Books.

Grabowsky, Volker 2008 'The Tai Polities in the Upper Mekong and Their Tributary Relationships with China and Burma', *Aséanie* 21. 11-63.

Grabowsky, Volker & Andrew Turton 2003 *The Gold and Silver Road of Trade and Friendship: The McLeod and Richardson Diplomatic Missions to Tai States in 1837*. Chiang Mai: Silkworm Books.

Gramsci, Antonio 1992, 1996 *Prison Notebooks*. (Vols. 1 & 2). New York: Columbia University Press.

– 1971 *Selections from the Prison Notebooks*. New York: International Publishers.

Haas, Mary R 1964 *Thai-English Student's Dictionary*. Stanford: Stanford University Press.

Hanks, Lucien M 1962 'Merit and Power in the Thai Social Order', *American Anthropologist* 64 (6). 1247-1261.

Hansen, Thomas 1997 'Inside the Romanticist Episteme', *Thesis Eleven* 48 (1). 21-41.

Hardt, Michael & Antonio Negri 2000 *Empire*. Cambridge, Mass: Harvard University Press.

Hart, Gillian, Andrew Turton & Benjamin White (ed.) 1989 *Agrarian Transformations: Local Processes and the State in Southeast Asia*. Berkeley: University of California Press.

Hevia, James L 1995 *Cherishing Men from Afar: Qing Guest Ritual and the Macartney Embassy of 1793*. Durham and London: Duke University Press.

Hewison, Kevin (ed.) 1997 *Political Change in Thailand: Democracy and Participation*. London and New York: Routledge.

– 2007 'Noam Chomsky on Indochina and Iraq: An Interview', *Journal of Contemporary Asia* 37 (4). 397-409.

Hewison, Kevin & Rodan, G. 1994 'Whatever Happened to the Revolution? The Declineof the Left in Southeast Asia', *Socialist Register 1994*. London: Merlin Press. 235-62.

Hindess, Barry & Paul Hirst 1975 *Pre-capitalist Modes of Production*. London and Boston: Routledge and Kegan Paul.

Hinton, Peter 2000 'Where Nothing is as It Seems: Between Southeast China and Mainland Southeast Asia in the "Post-Socialist" Era', in G. Evans, C. Hutton and Kuah Khun Eng (ed.) *Where China Meets Southeast Asia: Social and Cultural Change in Border Regions*. Bangkok: White Lotus; Singapore: Institute of Southeast Asian Studies.

Hirsch, Philip 1990 *Development dilemmas in rural Thailand*. Singapore: Oxford University Press.
– 1994 'The Thai countryside in the 1990s', *Southeast Asian Affairs 1994*. Singapore: Institute of Southeast Asian Affairs.
– 2001 'Globalisation, Regionalisation and Local Voices: The Asian Development Bank and Re-scaled Politics of the Environment in the Mekong Region', *Singapore Journal of Tropical Geography* 22 (3). 237-251.
Hirsch, Philip & Andrew Wyatt 2004 'Negotiating local livelihoods: Scales of conflict in the Se San River Basin', *Asia Pacific Viewpoint* 45(1). 51-68.

Ingram, James C. 1971 *Economic Change in Thailand, 1850-1970*. Stanford: Stanford University Press.
Isager, Lotte & Soren Ivarsson 2002 'Contesting landscapes in Thailand: Tree Ordination as Counter-Territorialization', *Critical Asian Studies* 34 (3). 395-417.
Ishii, Yoneo 1975 'A Note on Buddhistic Millenarian Revolts in Northeastern Siam', *Journal of Southeast Asian Studies* 6 (2). 121-126.

Jamaree Pitackwong (Chiengthong) 1996 Disorganized Development: Changing Forms of Work and Livelihood in Rural Northern Thailand. Unpublished Ph.D thesis, School of Oriental and African Studies, University of London.
Journal of Contemporary Asia (JCA). 1978. Special issue on Thailand: 'Roots of Conflict'.

Kasian Tejapira 2006 'Toppling Thaksin', *New Left Review* 39 (May/June). 5-37.
Kerkvliet, Ben 2002 *Everyday Politics in the Philippines: Class and Status Relations in a Central Luzon Village*. Lanham: Rowman and Littlefield.
– 2005 *The Power of Everyday Politics: How Vietnamese Peasants Transformed National Policy*. Ithaca: Cornell University Press.
Keyes, Charles F. 1967 *Isan: Regionalism in Northeastern Thailand* (Data Paper No. 65). Ithaca, NY: Cornell University Southeast Asia Program.
– 1973 'The Power of Merit', in *Visakha Puja B.E. 2516*. Bangkok: The Buddhist Association of Thailand, Annual Publication. 95102.
– 1977 'Millennialism, Theravāda Buddhism, and Thai Society', *Journal of Asian Studies*, 36 (2). 283302.
– 2002 'National Heroine or Local Spirit? The Struggle over Memory in the Case of Thao Suranari of Nakhon Ratchasima', in Shigeharu Tanabe & Charles Keyes (ed.) *Cultural Crisis and Social Memory: Modernity and Identity in Thailand and Laos*. Richmond: Routledge Curzon. 113-36.
– forthcoming 'Communism, Peasants and Buddhism: The Failure of "Peasant Revolutions" in Thailand in Comparison to Cambodia', in John Marston (ed.) *Community and the Trajectories of Change in Cambodia and Thailand: Anthropological Studies in Honor of May Ebihara*. (Under consideration for publication by the University of Washington Press together with Silkworm Press).
Klein, Martin A. (ed.) 1993 *Breaking the Chains: Slavery, Bondage, and Emancipation in Modern Africa and Asia*. Madison: University of Wisconsin Press.
Kolko, G. 2006 *After Socialism: Reconstructing Social Thought*. London and New York: Routledge.
Korff, Rudiger 2003 'Local enclosures of Globalization: The power of locality', *Dialectical Anthropology* 27. 1-18.
Krungthep Thurakit (2550 B.E.) (In Thai) 'Themasek positioning 3 strategies of investing abroad', 24 November 2007.

Kumar, Dharma 1993 'Colonialism, Bondage, and Caste in British India', in Klein, Martin A. (ed.). *Breaking the Chains: Slavery, Bondage, and Emancipation in Modern Africa and Asia*. Madison: University of Wisconsin Press. 112-130.

Laclau, Ernesto 1977 *Politics and Ideology in Marxist Thought: Capitalism – Fascism – Populism*. London: New Left Books.
Laclau, Ernesto & Chantal Mouffe 1985 (2nd ed. 2001) *Hegemony and socialist strategy: towards a radical democratic politics*. New York and London: Verso.
Lash, Scott 2006 'Life (Vitalism)', *Theory, Culture, and Society* 23 (2-3). 323-39.
– 2007 'Power after Hegemony', *Theory, Culture and Society* 24 (3). 55-78.
Lasker, Bruno 1950 *Human Bondage in Southeast Asia*. Chapel Hill: University of North Carolina Press.
Leach 1961 'Jingpaw Kinship Terminology', in his *Rethinking Anthropology*. London: The Athlone Press.
Levy, Pierre 1997 *Collective Intelligence: Mankind's Emerging World in Cyberspace*. New York: Plenum Trade.
Li, Tania 1999 'Compromising power: development, culture and rule in Indonesia', *Cultural Anthropology* 14(3). 295-322.
– 2005 'Beyond "the state" and failed schemes', *American Anthropologist* 107 (3). 383-394.
– 2007 *The will to improve: governmentality, development, and the practice of politics*. Durham: Duke University Press.
Liew-Herres, Foon Ming & Volker Grabowsky (in collaboration with Aroonrut Wichienkeeo) 2008 *Lan Na in Chinese Historiography: Sino-Tai Relations as Reflected in the Yuan and Ming Sources (13th to 17th Centuries)*. Bangkok: Institute of Asian Studies, Chulalongkorn University.
Liew-Herres, Foon Ming, Volker Grabowsky & Renoo Wichasin 2009 (forthcoming) *Chronicles of Sipsòng Panna: Translation and Analyses*. Chiang Mai: Silkworm Books.
Lingat, R. 1931 *L'esclavage privé dans le vieux droit siamois*. Paris: Les Editions Domat-Montchrestien.
Loos, Tamara 2006 *Subject Siam: Family, Law, and Colonial Modernity in Thailand*. Ithaca and London: Cornell University Press.

Ma Thaung 1954 British Interest in Trans-Burma Trade Routes to China 1826-1876. Unpub. Ph.D. thesis, School of Oriental and African Studies, University of London [OIOC Eur. MSS. C.129; and University of London Library, Senate House].
McCargo, Duncan 2005 'Network monarchy and legitimacy crises in Thailand', *The Pacific Review* 18 (4). 499-519.
– 2006 'Thaksin and the resurgence of violence in the Thai South: Network monarchy strikes back?', *Critical Asian Studies* 38 (1). 39-71.
– (ed.) 2007 *Rethinking Thailand's Southern Violence*. Singapore: National University of Singapore.
McCargo, Duncan & Ukrist Pathmanand 2005 *The Thaksinization of Thailand*. Copenhagen: Nordic Institute for Asian Studies Press.
McLeod, W.C. and D. Richardson 1869 'Copy of Papers relating to the route of Captain W.C. McLeod from Moulmein to the Frontiers of China, and to the Route of Dr. Richardson on his Fourth Mission to the Shan Provinces of Burmah, or Extracts from the Same' in [British] *Parliamentary Papers 1868/69*. Vol. 46. Paper No. 420. London: House of Commons [British Library, London, Oriental and India Office Collections].
McVey, Ruth (ed.). 2000 *Money & Power in Provincial Thailand*. Singapore, Copenhagen, Chiang Mai: Institute for Southeast Asian Studies, Institute for Asian Studies and Silkworm Books.

Maha Ammattayathibòdi, Phraya (พระยามหาอำมาตยธิบดี) 1963. พงศาวดารเมืองนคร เชียงใหม่ เมืองนครลำปาง เมืองลำพูนไชย [The Chronicle of Chiang Mai, Lampang and Lamphun]. In ประชุมพงศาวดาร [Collected Chronicles], Part 3, Vol. 3, pp. 87-131. Bangkok: Khurusapha.

Mallet, M. 1978 'Causes and Consequences of the October '76 Coup', *Journal of Contemporary Asia* 8 (1). 80-103.

Manas Chitakasem & Andrew Turton (ed.) 1991 *Thai Constructions of Knowledge. London: School of Oriental and African Studies, University of London.*

Michener, Victoria J. 1998 'The participatory approach: contradiction and co-option in Burkina Faso', *World Development* 26 (12). 2105-2118.

Missingham, Bruce 2004 *The Assembly of the Poor in Thailand: From Local Struggles to National Protest Movement.* Chiang Mai: Silkworm Books.

Moerman, Michael 1969 'The Thai Village Headman as a Synaptic Leader', *Journal of Asian Studies* 28 (3). 535-549.

Mosse, David 1994 'Authority, gender and knowledge: theoretical reflections on the practice of participatory rural appraisal', *Development and Change* 25. 497-526.

– 2001 ' "People's knowledge", participation and patronage: operations and representations in rural development', in Bill Cooke and Uma Kothari (ed.) *Participation: the new tyranny?* London: Zed Books. 16-35.

– 2005 *Cultivating development: an ethnography of aid policy and Practice.* London: Pluto Press.

Mouffe, Chantal (ed.) 1999 *The Challenge of Carl Schmitt.* London and New York: Verso.

Murdoch, John B 1974 'The 19011902 "Holy Man's" Rebellion', *Journal of the Siam Society* 62 (1). 4766.

Muscat, R 1994 *The Fifth Tiger: A Study of Thai Development Policy.* Helsinki and Armonk: United Nations University Press and M.E. Sharpe.

Naisbitt, John 1996 'Global Forces Shape Asia', *Far Eastern Economic Review Fiftieth Anniversary Commemorative Edition: Telling Asia's Story.* Hong Kong: Dow Jones.

Nancy, Jean-Luc 1994 'The Abandonment of Being' in his *The Birth to Presence.* Palo Alto: Stanford University Press.

Negri, Antonio 1991 *The Savage Anomaly: the power of Spinoza's metaphysics and politics.* Minneapolis: University of Minnesota Press.

NESDB (nd[a]) *The fifth national economic and social development plan (1982-1986).* Bangkok: National Economic and Social Development Board.

NESDB (nd[b]) *The sixth national economic and social development plan (1987-1991).* Bangkok: National Economic and Social Development Board.

NESDB (nd[c]) *The seventh national economic and social development plan (1992-1996).* Bangkok: National Economic and Social Development Board.

NESDB (nd[d]) *The eighth national economic and social development plan (1997-2001).* Bangkok: National Economic and Social Development Board.

NESDB (nd[e]) *The ninth national economic and social development plan (2002-2006).* Bangkok: National Economic and Social Development Board.

Nidhi Eoseewong 2003 'The Thai Cultural Constitution', *Kyoto Review of Southeast Asia.* http://kyotoreview.cseas.kyoto-u.ac.jp/issue/issue2/index.html. Accessed on 18 July 2008.

Nun & Cartier 1986 'Elements for a Theory of Democracy: Gramsci and Common Sense', *Boundary 2* 14 (3). 197-229.

Nygren, Anja 1999 'Local knowledge in the environment-development discourse: From dichotomies to situated knowledge', *Critique of Anthropology* 19 (3). 267-288.

Ockey, James 2004 *Making Democracy: Leadership, Class, Gender, and Political Participation in Thailand.* Chiang Mai: Silkworm Books.

Parkin, David, 1996 'Introduction: The Power of the Bizarre' in David Parkin, Lionel Caplan and Humphrey Fisher (ed.) *The Politics of Cultural Performance*. Oxford and Providence, R.I: Berghahn Books.

Pasuk Phongpaichit & Chris Baker 1996 *Thailand's Boom!* Chiang Mai: Silkworm Books.

– 2004 *Thaksin: The Business of Politics*. Chiangmai, Copenhagen: Silkworm Books, Nordic Institute for Asian Studies.

– 2008 'Thakin's Populism', *Journal of Contemporary Asia* 38 (1). 62-83.

Pasuk Phongpaichit & Sungsidh Phiriyarangsan 1994 *Corruption and Democracy in Thailand*. Bangkok: Political Economy Centre, Faculty of Economics, Chulalongkorn University.

Pattana Kittiarsa 2001 'Making Sense of Modernity: *Mawlam Cing* and Everyday Life Experience in Northeast Thai Villages', paper presented at international symposium on 'Everyday Life Experience of Modernity in Thailand: An Ethnographic Approach,' sponsored by the Japan Society for Promotion of Science, Chiang Mai, Thailand.

– 2005 '"Lives of Hunting Dogs": *Muay Thai* and the Politics of Thai Masculinities', *South East Asia Research* 13 (1). 57-90.

– 2006 'The Romance of Overseas Migrant Workers: Popular Music and the Transformation of Cultural Intimacies in Northeastern Thailand.' Singapore, ms.

– 2009a 'The Lyrics of Laborious Life: Popular Music and the Reassertion of Migrant Manhood in Thailand', *Inter-Asia Cultural Studies* 10 (3). 381-98.

– 2009b 'Nostalgic Parodies and Migrant Ironies in Two Comedy Films', paper presented at the international conference on 'Filmic Interventions in Contemporary Southeast Asia' organised by Center for Integrated Area Studies, Kyoto University, 13-15 November.

– 2009c '*Dontrī Īsān, raēngnān ārom, lae khonphalangthin* [Popular Music, Emotional Labor, and Isan Diaspora].' Singapore, ms.

Patterson, Orlando 1982 *Of Human Bondage. Slavery and Social Death: A Comparative Study*. Cambridge, Mass: Harvard University Press.

Ploger, John 2006 'In Search of Urban Vitality', *Space and Culture* 9. 382-99.

Polanyi, Karl 1957 *The Great Transformation: The Political and Economic Origin of Our Time*. Boston: Beacon Press.

Pottier, Johan, Alan Bicker & Paul Sillitoe (ed.) 2003 *Negotiating Local Knowledge: Power and Identity in Development*. London: Pluto Press.

Prachakitcakòracak, Phraya (พระยาประชากิจกรจักร) 1973 [1907]. พงศาวดารโยนก [The Yonok Chronicle] 7th edition. Bangkok: Khlang witthaya.

Prakash, Gyan 1990 *Bonded Histories: Genealogies of Labor Servitude in Colonial India*. Cambridge, New York, Melbourne: Cambridge University Press.

– 1993 'Terms of Servitude: The colonial Discourse on Slavery and Bondage in India', in Klein, Martin A. (ed.) 1993 *Breaking the Chains: Slavery, Bondage, and Emancipation in Modern Africa and Asia*. Madison: University of Wisconsin Press. 131-149.

Pratt, Mary Louise 1992 *Imperial Eyes: Travel Writing and Transculturation*. London and New York: Routledge.

Reid, Anthony 1983a ' "Closed" and "Open" Slave Systems in Pre-colonial Southeast Asia,' in his (ed.) *Slavery, Bondage and Dependency in Southeast Asia*. St. Lucia, London and New York: University of Queensland Press. 156-181.

– (ed.) 1983b *Slavery, Bondage and Dependency in Southeast Asia*. St. Lucia, London and New York: University of Queensland Press.

Resurreccion, Bernadette, Mary Jane Real & Panadda Pantana 2004 'Officialising strategies and gender in Thailand's water resources sector', *Development in Practice* 14 (4). 521-533.

Reynolds, Craig J. 1979 'Monastery Lands and Labor Endowments in Thailand: Some Effects of Social and Economic Change, 1868-1910', *Journal of the Economic and Social History of the Orient* 22 (2). 190-227.

– 1991 'Sedition in Thai history: a nineteenth century poem and its critics', in Manas Chitakasem & Andrew Turton (ed.) *Thai Constructions of Knowledge*. London: School of Oriental and African Studies.

– 1992 'The Plot of Thai History: Theory and Practice', in Gehan Wijeyewardene & Edward Chapman (ed.) *Patterns and Illusions: Thai History and Thought (In Memory of Richard Davis)*. Canberra: The Richard Davis Foundation and Department of Anthropology, RSPAS, Australian National University.

– 2002 'Introduction: National Identity and Its Defenders', in his (ed.) *National Identity and Its Defenders: Thailand Today*. Chiangmai: Silkworm Books.

– 2003 'Tai-land and its Others', *South East Asia Research* 11 (1). 113-130.

– 2007 *Jaosua khunsoek saktina panyachon lae khonsaman ruapruam botkhwam prawattisat khong khrek je renon [Tycoons, Warlords, Feudalists Intellectuals, and Ordinary Folks: Collected Essays on History by Craig J. Reynolds]*, ed. and trans., Waruni Otsatharom. Bangkok: Textbook Project, Thammasat University.

Reynolds, Craig J. & Hong Lysa 1983 'Marxism in Thai Historical Studies', *Journal of Asian Studies* 43 (1). 77-104.

Richardson, David 1829-35 'Journals of Missions from Tenasserim to the Chiefs of the Shan States in Siam in 1829-30 and 1834-35; and a visit to Ava 1830-31'. Add. 30.354 [British Library, London, Western Manuscript Department].

Rigg, Jonathan 2001 *More than the Soil: Rural Change in Southeast Asia*. Harlow: Pearson Education Ltd.

– 2003 *Southeast Asia: The Human Landscape of Modernization and Development*. London and New York: Routledge.

Rigg, Jonathan, Anna Allott, Rachel Harrison & Ukruch Kratz 1999 'Understanding languages of modernisation', *Modern Asian Studies* 33 (3). 581-602

Rigg, Jonathan & Albert Salamanca 2009 'Managing risk and vulnerability in Asia: A (re) study from Thailand, 1982-83 and 2008', *Asia Pacific Viewpoint* 50 (3). 255-270.

Sāimöng Mangrai, Sao 1965 *The Shan states and the British annexation* (Data Paper No. 57). Ithaca: Cornell University Southeast Asia Program.

– 1981 *The Pādaeng Chronicle and the Jengtung State Chronicle Translated*. Ann Arbor: Center for South and Southeast Asian Studies, University of Michigan.

Saipin Kaewngarmprasert (Sāipin Kāēongāmprasoet) 1995 *Kānmüang nai anusāwarī Thāo Suranārī* (The Politics of the Monument of Thāo Suranārī). Bangkok: Matichon, Sinlapawatthanatham Chabap Phisēt, 2538.

Sangsit Piriyarangsan & Phasuk Pongpaijit (2536 B.E.) (In Thai) *Chon Chan Klang Bon Krasae Prachathipatai Thai*. Bangkok: Centre of Politcal Economy Study, Chulalongkorn University.

Sanit Samuckakorn (2539B.E.) (In Thai) *Mii Ngoen Kau Nub Wa Nong, Mii Thong Kau Nub wa Pii*. Bangkok: Academic Paper Division, NIDA.

Saraswadee Ongsakul (สรัสวดี อ่องสกุล) 1991 จดหมายเหตุล้านนา บันทึกเหตุการณ์ ประวัติศาสตร์ พ.ศ. 2271-2397 [Records of Lan Na: Notes of Historical Events, A.D. 1728-1854]. In หลักฐานประวัติศาสตร์ล้านนา จากเอกสารคัมภีร์ใบลาน และ พับหนังสา [Historical Sources of Lan Na from Palmleaf and Mulberry Paper Manuscripts]. Chiang Mai: Chiang Mai University. 12-37.

Schmitt, Carl (1922) 1985 *Political Theology: Four Chapters on the Concept of Sovereignty*. Cambridge, Mass: MIT Press.

Schomburgk, Robert H. 1863 'A Visit to Xiengmai, the Principal City of the Laos or Shan States', *Journal of the Royal Asiatic Society of Bengal* 32. 387-99.

Schwartz, Stuart B. 1994 *Implicit Understandings: Observing, Reporting, and Reflecting on the Encounters Between Europeans and other Peoples in the Early Modern Era*. Cambridge: Cambridge University Press.

Scott, James 1976 *The Moral Economy of the Peasant: rebellion and subsistence in Southeast Asia.* New Haven: Yale University Press.

– 1985 *Weapons of the Weak: Everyday Forms of Peasant Resistance.* New Haven: Yale University Press.

Smyth, H. Warington (1898) 1994 *Five Years in Siam, from 1891 to 1896,* 2 vols, with an introduction by Tamara Loos. New York: Charles Scribner's Sons [reprinted 1994, Bangkok: White Lotus].

Somchai Patharathananunth 2006 *Civil Society and Democratization: Social Movements in Northeast Thailand.* Copenhagen: Nordic Institute for Asian Studies Press.

– 2008 'The Thai Rak Thai Party and Elections in Northeastern Thailand,' *Journal of Contemporary Asia* 38 (1). 105-123.

Somjai Phirotthirarach 1983 The Historical Writings of Chao Phraya Thiphakorawong. Unpub. Ph.D. thesis, Northern Illinois University.

Sperber, Dan 1975 *Rethinking Symbolism.* Cambridge: Cambridge University Press.

– 1985 *On Anthropological Knowledge: three essays.* Cambridge: Cambridge University Press.

Spivak, Gayatri 1988a 'Can the Subaltern Speak?' in Cary Nelson & Lawrence Grossberg (ed.) *Marxism and the Interpretation of Culture.* Urbana: University of Illinois Press.

– 1988b *Other Worlds: Essays in Cultural Politics.* London and New York: Routledge.

Sunthari Asawai 1987 *Prawat khlong rangsit kan phatthana thidin lae phonkrathop to sangkhom, pho so 2431-2457 [A History of the Rangsit Canals: Land Development Its Social Impact].* Bangkok: Textbook Project, Thammasat University Press.

Tambiah, Stanley 1970 *Buddhism and the Spirit Cults in Northeast Thailand.* Cambridge, London and New York: Cambridge University Press.

Tanabe, Shigeharu 1984 'Ideological Practice in Peasant Rebellions: Siam at the Turn of the Twentieth Century', in Andrew Turton & Shigeharu Tanabe (ed.) *History and Peasant Consciousness in South East Asia* (Senri Ethnological Studies 13). Osaka: National Museum of Ethnology. 75-100.

Tej Bunnag 1967 'Khabot phū mī bun phāk Īsān R.S. 121' (Millenarian Revolt in Northeastern Thailand, 1902), *Sangkhomsāt parithat* (Social Science Review) 5 (1). 7886.

– 1968. 'Khabot ngiao müang Phrāē' (Shan Rebellion in Müang Phrae), *Sangkhomsāt parithat* (Social Science Review) 6 (2). 6782.

– 1977 *The Provincial Administration of Siam, 18921915.* Kuala Lumpur: Oxford University Press.

– 1981 *Khabot R.S. 121* (1902 Rebellions). Bangkok: Mūnnithi Khrōngkān Tamrā Sang khomsāt lae Manutsāt, 2524.

Terwiel, Barend 1983 'Bondage and Slavery in Early Nineteenth Century Siam', in Anthony Reid (ed.). *Slavery, Bondage and Dependency in Southeast Asia.* St. Lucia, London and New York: University of Queensland Press. 118-137.

– 1984 'Formal Structure and Informal Rules: An Historical Perspective on Hierarchy, Bondage and the Patron-Client Relationship', in Han ten Brummelhuis & Jeremy H. Kemp (ed.) *Strategies and Structures in Thai Society.* Amsterdam: Anthropological-Sociological Centre, University of Amsterdam. 19-38.

Thailand 1969 [1936]. เรื่องทูตฝรั่ง สมัยกรุงรัตนโกสินทร์ [Records of European Embassies in the Early Bangkok Period]. In ประชุมพงศาวดาร [Collected Chronicles], Part 62, Vol. 34. Bangkok: Khurusapha.

Thailand 1961 Khanakammakan phatthana tawanôkchiang nüa. Phaen phatthana phatthana tawanôkchiang nüa Ph.S. 2505-2509 [Northeast Development Plan, 1962-1966]. Bangkok: Suan Wang Phang Phatthanakansetthakit, Samnakngan Satha Phatthanasetthakit haeng Chat, Samnak Nayok Ratthamontri. 2504.

Thailand n.d. The Committee on Development of the Northeast. [1961]. The Northeast Development Plan, 1962-1966. Bangkok: The Planning Office, the National Economic Development Board, Office of the Prime Minister.

Thak Chaloemtiarana (ed). 1978. *Thai Politics: Extracts and Documents, 19321957*. Bangkok: The Social Science Association of Thailand.

Thawi Sawangpanyangkun (ทวี สว่างปัญญางกูร) 1984. ตำนานเมืองยอง [Müang Yòng Chronicle]. Chiang Mai: Chiang Mai University.

– 1990 พงสาวดารเมืองเชียงตุง [Chiang Tung Chronicle]. Cremation volume for Cao Mae Thipphawan na Chiang Tung. Chiang Mai.

Therborn, Göran 1980 *The Ideology of Power and the Power of Ideology*. London: New Left Books.

Thiphakòrawong, Caophraya (เจ้าพระยาทิพากรวงศ์) 1961 พระราชพงศาวดารกรุง รัตนโกสินทร์ รัชกาลที่ ๓ [The Royal Chronicle of the Bangkok Era Third Reign] 2 vols. Bangkok: Khurusapha.

Thitinan Phongsudirak 1997 'Thailand's Media: Whose Watchdog?' in Kevin Hewison (ed.) *Political Change in Thailand: Democracy and Participation*. London and New York: Routledge.

Thompson, E.P. 1968 *The Making of the English Working Classes. Harmondsworth: Penguin Books*.

Thompson, Virginia 1941 *Thailand: The New Siam*. New York: Macmillan for the Secretariat, Institute of Pacific Relation, International Research Service.

Thongchai Winichakul 1994 *Siam Mapped: A History of the Geo-Body of a Nation*. Chiang Mai: Silkworm Books.

– 2000 'The Others Within: Travel and Ethno-Spatial Differentiation of Siamese Subjects 1885-1910', in Andrew Turton (ed.) *Civility and Savagery: Social Identity in Tai States*. Richmond: Curzon Press.

– 2002 'Remembering/Silencing the Traumatic Past: The Ambivalence Narratives of the October 1976 Massacre in Thailand', in Shigeharu Tanabe & Charles Keyes (ed.) *Cultural Crisis and Social Memory: Modernity and Identity in Thailand and Laos*. London: RoutledgeCurzon.

– 2008 'Toppling Democracy', *Journal of Contemporary Asia* 38 (1). 11-37.

Toledano, Ehud R. 1993 'Ottoman Concepts of Slavery in the Period of Reform, 1830s-1880s', in Klein, Martin A. (ed.) *Breaking the Chains: Slavery, Bondage, and Emancipation in Modern Africa and Asia*. Madison: University of Wisconsin Press. 37-63.

Turnbull, David 1997 'Reframing science and other local knowledge traditions,' *Futures* 29 (6). 551-562.

Turton, Andrew 1972 'Matrilineal descent groups and spirit cults of the Thai-yuan in northern Thailand', *Journal of the Siam Society* 60 (2). 217-56.

– 1976a 'Northern Thai Peasant Society: Twentieth-Century Transformations in Political and Jural Structures', *Journal of Peasant Studies* 3 (3). 267-298.

– 1976b Northern Thai Peasant Society: A Case Study of Jural and Political Structures at the Village Level and Their Twentieth Century Transformations. Unpub. Ph.D. thesis, School of Oriental and African Studies, University of London.

– 1978a 'The Current Situation in the Thai countryside', in Andrew Turton, Jonathan Fast & Malcolm Caldwell (ed.) *Thailand: Roots of Conflict*. Nottingham: Spokesman Books.

– 1978b 'Architectural and Political Space in Thailand', in George Milner (ed.) *Natural Symbols in Southeast Asia*. London: School of Oriental and African Studies.

– 1980 'Thai Institutions of Slavery,' in James L. Watson (ed.) *Asian and African Systems of Slavery*. Oxford: Basil Blackwell. 251-292. Rev. ed. in Condominas (ed.) 1998.

– 1984 'Limits of Ideological Domination and the Formation of Social Consciousness', in Andrew Turton & Shigeharu Tanabe (ed.) *History and Peasant Consciousness in Southeast Asia* (Senri Ethnological Studies 13). Osaka: National Museum of Ethnology. 19-73.

– 1986 'Patrolling the Middle-Ground: Methodological Perspectives on "Everyday Peasant Resistance"', *Journal of Peasant Studies* 13 (2). (Special Issue on Everyday Forms of Peasant Resistance in South-East Asia, ed. James C. Scott & Benedict J. Tria Kerkvliet). 36-48.

– 1987 *Production, power and participation in rural Thailand: experiences of poor farmers' groups*, Geneva: United Nations Research Institute for Social Development.

– 1988 'Ideological Commodity Production' in John G. Taylor & Andrew Turton (ed.) *Sociology of 'Developing Societies': Southeast Asia*. Basingstoke: Macmillan.

– 1989a 'Local Powers and Rural Differentiation', in G.P. Hart, A. Turton & B. White (ed.) *Agrarian Transformations: Local Processes and the State in Southeast Asia*. Berkeley: University of California Press. 70-97.

– 1989b 'Thailand: Agrarian Bases of State Power', in G.P. Hart, A. Turton & B. White (ed.) *Agrarian Transformations: Local Processes and the State in Southeast Asia*. Berkeley: University of California Press. 53-69.

– 1991a 'Invulnerability and Local Knowledge', in Manas Chitakasem & Andrew Turton (ed.) *Thai Constructions of Knowledge*. London: School of Oriental and African Studies, University of London. 155-182.

– 1991b 'State Poetics and Civil Rhetoric: an introduction to Thai Constructions of Knowledge', in Manas Chitakasem & Andrew Turton (ed.) *Thai Constructions of Knowledge*. London: School of Oriental and African Studies, University of London. 1-14.

– 1997 'Ethnography of embassy: anthropological readings of records of diplomatic encounters between Britain and Tai states in the early nineteenth century', *South East Asia Research*, 5 (2). 175-205.

– 1998a Diplomatic Missions to Tai states by David Richardson and W.C. McLeod 1830-1839: Anthropological Perspectives', *Journal of the Siam Society*. 86, Parts 1 & 2. 9-25.

– 1998b 'Thai Institutions of Slavery', in Georges Condominas (ed.) *Formes extrêmes de dépendance: contributions à l'étude de l'esclavage en Asie du Sud-Est*. Paris: Editions de l'École des Hautes Études en Sciences Sociales. 411-57.

– 1999 'Diplomatic missions to Tai states by David Richardson and W.C. McLeod 1830-1839', *Journal of the Siam Society* 86 (1, 2). 9-25.

– (ed.) 2000 *Civility and Savagery: Social Identity in Tai States*. Richmond: Curzon Press.

– 2001 'Delay and deception in Tai-British diplomatic encounters of the early 19th century', in Joy Hendry & C.W. Watson (ed.) *An anthropology of indirect communication* (ASA Monographs 37). London: Routledge. 271-89.

– 2004 'Violent Capture of People for Exchange on Karen-Tai Borders in the 1830s', in Gwyn Campbell (ed.) *The Structure of Slavery in Indian Ocean Africa and Asia*. London: Cass. 69-82.

– 2006 'Remembering Local History: Kuba Wajiraphanya (c.1853-1928), Phra Thongthip and the *Muang* Way of Life', *Journal of the Siam Society* 94. 147-176.

– 2007 Review of G.J. Younghusband's *The Trans-Salween Shan State of Kian Tiung*, in *Journal of the Siam Society*. 95. 224-28.

Turton, Andrew, Jonathan Fast & Malcolm Caldwell (ed.) 1978 *Thailand: Roots of Conflict*. Nottingham: Spokesman Books. *Journal of Contemporary Asia* 8 (1). 104-142.

Turton, Andrew & Shigeharu Tanabe (ed.) 1984a *History and Peasant Consciousness in South East Asia*. Osaka: National Museum of Ethnology.

Turton, Andrew & Shigeharu Tanabe 1984b 'Introduction' to Andrew Turton & Shigeharu Tanabe (ed.) *History and Peasant Consciousness in Southeast Asia* (Senri Ethnological Studies 13). Osaka: National Museum of Ethnology.

Ubonrat Siriyuvasak 2007 'New media for Civil Society and Political Censorship in Thailand', *AsiaRights Journal* 8. (Online journal; http://rspas.anu.edu.au/asiarightsjournal/).

Ukrist Pathmanand 2008 'A Different Coup D'État?' *Journal of Contemporary Asia* 38 (1). 124-142.

UNDP 2007 *Thailand human development report 2007: sufficiency economy and human develop-ment*, Bangkok : UNDP. http://hdr.undp.org/en/reports/nationalreports/asiathepacific/thai-land/name,3418,en.html.

Ungapakorn, Giles Ji 1997 *The Struggle for Democracy and Social Justice in Thailand* Bangkok: Arom Pongpangan Foundation.

— 2007 *A Coup for the Rich: Thailand's Political Crisis.* Bangkok: Workers Democracy Publish-ing.

Vajiravudh, King 1951 'Kankha yingsao [On the Trade in Young Women],' in *Pramuan bot phratchaniphon nai phrabat somdet phramongkut klao jaoyuhua [Collected Essays of King Vajir-avudh].* Bangkok. Cremation volume for Phraya Aniruthewa (M.L. Phun Phoengbun). 53-59.

Vandergeest, Peter 1993 'Constructing Thailand: Regulation, Everyday Resistance, and Citi-zenship, *Comparative Studies in Society and History* 35 (1).

— 2008 'New Concepts, New Natures?: Revisiting Commodities Production in Southern Thailand', in Joseph Nevins & Nancy Lee Peluso (ed.) *Taking Southeast Asia to Market: Commodities, People, and Nature in a Neoliberal Age.* Ithaca, NY: Cornell University Press.

Wakin, Eric 1992 *Anthropology Goes to War: Professional Ethics and Counterinsurgency in Thai-land.* Madison: Center for Southeast Asian Studies, University of Wisconsin.

Walker, Andrew 2001 'The "Karen Consensus": Ethnic Politics and Resource-Use Legitimacy in Northern Thailand', *Asian Ethnicity.* 2 (2). 145-62.

— 2004 'Response', *Asian Ethnicity.* 5 (2). 259-65.

— 2008 'The Rural Constitution and the Everyday Politics of Elections in Northern Thailand', *Journal of Contemporary Asia* 38 (1). 84-105.

Wallerstein, I., Fox-Keller, E., Juma, C., Kocka, J., Lecourt, D., Mudimbe, V.Y., Mushikoje, K., Prigogine, I., Taylor, P. & Trouillot, M.R. 1996 *Open the Social Sciences: Report of the Gul-benkian Commission on the Restructuring of the Social Sciences.* Stanford: Stanford University Press.

Wikipedia 2008 "H. Bruce Franklin," http://en.wikipedia.org/wiki/H._Bruce_Franklin, ac-cessed 3 October.

Williams, Raymond 1961 *The Long Revolution.* London: Chatto and Windus.

— 1977 *Marxism and Literature.* London and New York: Oxford University Press.

— 1980 *Problems in Materialism and Culture: Selected Essays.* London and New York: Verso.

Wilson, Constance M. 1997 'The Holy Man in the History of Thailand and Laos,' *Journal of Southeast Asian Studies* 28 (2). 345-64.

Wilson, David A. 1962 *Politics in Thailand.* Ithaca, NY: Cornell University Press.

Winai Pongsripian (วินัย พงศ์ศรีเพียร) 1999 (ed.) จดหมายเหตุนครเชียงใหม่ [Historical Records of Chiang Mai]. Bangkok: Prime Minister's Office.

Woodman, Dorothy 1962 *The Making of Burma.* London: Crescent Press.

Woods, Michael 2007 'Engaging the global countryside: Globalization, hybridity and the re-construction of rural place', *Progress in Human Geography* 3 (4). 485-507.

Wright, Sarah 2005 'Knowing scale: Intellectual property rights, knowledge space and the production of the global', *Social and Cultural Geography* 6 (6). 903-921.

Wyatt, David K. & Aroonrut Wichienkeeo 1995 *The Chiang Mai Chronicle.* Chiang Mai: Silk-worm Books.

Xin Liu 1998 'Yao: the Practice of Everyday Life in Northern Rural Shaanxi', in Wen-hsin Yeh (ed.) *Landscape, Culture and Power in Chinese Society.* Berkeley: Institute of East Asian Stu-dies, University of California.

Yoshinori Nishizaki 2007 'Constructing Moral Authority in Rural Thailand: Banharn Silpa-acha's Non-Violent War on Drugs', *Asian Studies Review* 31 (3). 343-64.

Younghusband, G. J. 2005 [1888]. *The Trans-Salwin Shan State of Kiang Tung*, edited with an introduction and glossary by David K. Wyatt. Chiang Mai: Silkworm Books.

Yukti Mukdawijit (2538 B.E.) (in Thai) *Kan Kau Tua Khong Krasae Wattanatham Chumchon Nai Sangkhom Thai B.E. 2520 2537*. M.A.dissertation, Faculty of Sociology and Anthropology, Thammasat University.

Index

 **P**UBLICATIONS **S**ERIES

Monographs

Marleen Dieleman
*The Rhythm of Strategy. A Corporate Biography of the Salim Group
of Indonesia*
Monographs 1
2007 (ISBN 978 90 5356 033 4)

Sam Wong
*Exploring 'Unseen' Social Capital in Community Participation. Everyday
Lives of Poor Mainland Chinese Migrants in Hong Kong*
Monographs 2
2007 (ISBN 978 90 5356 034 1)

Diah Ariani Arimbi
*Reading Contemporary Indonesian Muslim Women Writers. Representation,
Identity and Religion of Muslim Women in Indonesian Fiction*
Monographs 3
2009 (ISBN 978 90 8964 089 5)

Euis Nurlaelawati
*Modernization, Tradition and Identity. The Kompilasi Hukum Islam and
Legal Practice in the Indonesian Religious Courts*
Monographs 4
2010 (ISBN 978 90 8964 088 8)

Edited Volumes

Sebastian Bersick, Wim Stokhof and Paul van der Velde (eds.)
*Multiregionalism and Multilateralism. Asian-European Relations in a
Global Context*
Edited Volumes 1
2006 (ISBN 978 90 5356 929 0)

Khun Eng Kuah-Pearce (ed.)
Chinese Women and the Cyberspace
Edited Volumes 2
2008 (ISBN 978 90 5356 751 7)

Milan J. Titus and Paul P.M. Burgers (eds.)
*Rural Livelihoods, Resources and Coping with Crisis in Indonesia. A
    Comparative Study*
Edited Volumes 3
2008 (ISBN 978 90 8964 055 0)

Marianne Hulsbosch, Elizabeth Bedford and Martha Chaiklin (eds.)
Asian Material Culture
Edited Volumes 4
2009 (ISBN 978 90 8964 090 1)

Hans Hägerdal (ed.)
Responding to the West. Essays on Colonial Domination and Asian Agency
Edited Volumes 5
2009 (ISBN 978 90 8964 093 2)

Derek Heng and Syed Muhd Khairudin Aljunied (eds.)
Reframing Singapore. Memory – Identity – Trans-Regionalism
Edited Volumes 6
2009 (ISBN 978 90 8964 094 9)

Friederike Assandri and Dora Martins (eds.)
From Early Tang Court Debates to China's Peaceful Rise
Edited Volumes 7
2009 (ISBN 978 90 5356 795 1)

Erich Kolig, Vivienne SM. Angeles and Sam Wong (eds.)
*Identity in Crossroad Civilisations. Ethnicity, Nationalism and Globalism in
    Asia*
Edited Volumes 8
2009 (ISBN 978 90 8964 127 4)

Khun Eng Kuah-Pearce and Gilles Guiheux (eds.)
*Social Movements in China and Hong Kong. The Expansion of Protest
    Space*
Edited Volumes 9
2009 (ISBN 978 90 8964 131 1)

Huhua Cao (ed.)
Ethnic Minorities and Regional Development in Asia. Reality and Challenges
Edited Volumes 10
2009 (ISBN 978 90 8964 091 8)

M. Parvizi Amineh (ed.)
State, Society and International Relations in Asia. Reality and Challenges
Edited Volumes 11
2010 (ISBN 978 90 5356 794 4)

Philip F. Williams (ed.)
Asian Literary Voices. From Marginal to Mainstream
Edited Volumes 12
2010 (ISBN 978 90 8964 092 5)